TEACHING THE BLACK EXPERIENCE

Methods and Materials

JAMES A. BANKS, Ph.D.

College of Education
University of Washington, Seattle

fp

Fearon Publishers
Lear Siegler, Inc., Education Division
Belmont, California

237106

Preface

"When should I begin teaching about the Negro and race relations?"
  "What methods can I use to teach black history?"
  "What resources are available for teaching the black experience? How can I obtain them?"
  "Should I teach black history as a separate subject or as a part of regular social studies units?"

These are the kinds of questions that concerned teachers frequently ask the author when he conducts workshops on teaching the black experience. Such questions and concerns prompted the writing of this book. It was written to help the classroom teacher develop the teaching strategies and methods needed to teach the black experience and to lead the teacher to the needed resources. School districts throughout the nation have conducted special workshops on teaching black history. They have hired consultants on black studies and they have purchased many multiethnic teaching materials. In spite of these efforts, teachers are still searching for the most promising way to teach this controversial and significant subject.

A flood of materials on the black experience have been produced in recent years. Abundant materials, however, do not in themselves solve the classroom teacher's pedagogical problems. He must determine *how* the materials can be most effectively used to attain the objectives he has formulated. This book is primarily concerned with *methods* and *approaches* that can be used to create an effective learning environment for the study of race relations and the black experience in America.

The first chapter establishes a rationale for teaching the black experience. The research reviewed in this chapter documents the negative racial attitudes that children typically bring to school, and suggests the urgent need for the school to assume a major responsibility for helping students to develop more positive racial attitudes.

Chapter 2 explores ways to help the teacher organize lessons on the black experience and to determine their relationship to the regular school curriculum. Techniques for formulating clearly stated behavioral objectives, effective learning experiences, and methods of sound evaluation are also included in this chapter.

Chapters 3 through 6 present promising approaches to teaching the various historical periods. The chapters are presented within a historical framework because most social studies programs still have a historical emphasis and focus. However, the teacher who uses a different curriculum organizational pattern will also find these approaches helpful. Although each chapter presents a different approach to teaching the various periods, the methods presented for one historical period may also be used to teach other periods. For example, simulation, which is discussed in Chapter 5 in relation to the Reconstruction Period, can also be used to teach the civil rights movement or any other major topic. One major teaching strategy is described in each of these chapters.

The final chapter of the book is a bibliography which annotates resources for teaching the black experience.

The author is grateful to the many classroom teachers with whom he has worked in workshops throughout the nation for listening to and reacting to many of the ideas and suggestions offered in this volume. It was primarily they who convinced him that there was a need for a book such as this one. He is also grateful to The National Council for the Social Studies for permission to use his article, "Relevant Social Studies for Black Pupils," which appeared in *Social Education* in January, 1969. Parts of Chapter 1 are based on this article. Finally, I am deeply grateful to my wife, Cherry McGee Banks, for her unusual patience and support while I worked on the manuscript, for creating the simulation game described in this volume, and for writing most of Chapter 5.

JAMES A. BANKS
Seattle, Washington

Contents

1

The Need for
Intergroup Education

Our nation is involved in a racial crisis, one that has been marked by violent outbreaks in our cities and by the assassinations of civil rights leaders. The Report of the National Advisory Commission on Civil Disorders documents the racial polarization that is occurring in the nation. This crisis has permeated our public elementary and junior high schools. In a number of urban areas white and black students have clashed. Black students have boycotted classes and openly expressed hostility toward white teachers and administrators. In its controversial report, the National Advisory Commission on Civil Disorders illuminated this racial schism:

> . . . Our nation is moving toward two societies, one white, one black—separate and unequal. . . . the most fundamental [cause of the riots] is the racial attitude and behavior of white Americans toward black Americans. . . . Race prejudice has shaped our history decisively; it now threatens to affect our future. . . . White racism is essentially responsible for the explosive mixture which has been accumulating in our cities since the end of World War II.[1]

[1]*Report of the National Advisory Commission on Civil Disorders* (New York: Bantam Books, 1968), pp. 1 and 10.

1

Perhaps these words would have been easily dismissed if they had been written by a committee of recognized critics. However, they significantly affected the thinking of many Americans because they came from a respected commission appointed by President Lyndon B. Johnson.

In taking decisive steps to help relieve racial conflict and to help children develop more positive racial attitudes, educators have embarked upon a new frontier. Historically, the public schools have supported and perpetuated the dominant societal attitudes toward ethnic and cultural minorities. Most educators now realize that unless we play a leading and decisive role in creating racial harmony and minimizing polarization our democracy will face a momentous challenge with which it may be incapable of coping.

RESEARCH INTO CHILDREN'S RACIAL ATTITUDES

In recent years, research in the behavioral sciences has documented the urgent need for both black and white children to develop more positive racial attitudes. This research has illuminated the negative racial attitudes held by all children and revealed the deflated self-concepts that black children typically manifest. Research by Clark and Clark in 1950 documented the negative and confused racial attitudes frequently expressed by black children.[2] The black subjects who participated in the Clarks' studies usually expressed a preference for white dolls and they rejected black dolls. Their preference of white to black was candid and explicit. These children also evidenced a tendency to avoid realistic self-identification. The Clarks note that "It is clear that the Negro child by age five is aware of the fact that to be colored in contemporary American society is a mark of inferior status. This apparently introduces a fundamental conflict at the very foundation of the ego structure." In research conducted in 1952, Goodman found that black children under age five frequently manifest uneasiness because of their awareness of skin-color differences.[3] In a study conducted by Morland in 1962, the Clark findings were confirmed. Rather than using dolls, Morland showed kindergarten children pictures of black and white children and asked them which

[2]Kenneth B. Clark and Mamie P. Clark, "Emotional Factors in Racial Identification and Preference in Negro Children," *Journal of Negro Education,* 19 (1950), pp. 341–50.

[3]Mary Ellen Goodman, *Race Awareness in Young Children* (Cambridge, Mass.: Addison Wesley, 1952), pp. 2–25.

children they would prefer for playmates. A majority of the subjects expressed a preference for white playmates. Morland concluded:

> A preference for whites was shown by a majority of subjects, including the youngest. . . . This indicates that preference for whites by children of both races developed early, even before racial differences could be communicated. Such results can be interpreted to mean that learning to prefer whites comes through "indirect" rather than "direct" verbal instruction.[4]

In 1965, Grossack replicated the 1950 study by the Clarks. He reports that most of the black children in his study expressed a preference for white dolls as opposed to black ones.[5]

Research indicates that black children not only express self-rejection and negative racial attitudes, but they tend to have low self-concepts. In 1963, Keller compared the self-concepts of black and white fifth grade children. She found that black children express more negative self-evaluations than white children.[6] The fact that black children typically have lower self-concepts than white children is especially significant since research indicates that children with low self-concepts of ability will not achieve at high levels.[7] Low self-concepts not only affect children's emotional adjustment but also their academic achievement.

Research conducted by this writer indicates that black children not only tend to express negative self-evaluations and racial attitudes, but that they often express hostility toward whites. In a study of fifth grade urban children, I found that the children had internalized many of the pervasive stereotypes of blacks, and that they also expressed hate as well as admiration for whites. I interpreted these findings to mean that the racial attitudes of black children are confused and conflicting since they devalued blacks, and expressed admiration for as well as hostility toward whites.

Research suggests that white children also come to the school with negative racial attitudes, even in kindergarten. After studying the

[4]J. Kenneth Morland, "Racial Acceptance and Preference of Nursery School Children in a Southern City," *Merrill-Palmer Quarterly of Behavior and Development,* 8 (1962), p. 279.

[5]Martin M. Grossack, "Psychological Considerations Essential to Effective Educational Integration," *Journal of Negro Education,* 35 (Summer 1965), pp. 278–87.

[6]Suzanne Keller, "The Social World of the Slum Child: Some Early Findings," *American Journal of Orthopsychiatry,* 33 (1963), pp. 823–31.

[7]Wilbur B. Brookover, Ann Paterson, and Shailer Thomas, "Self-concept of Ability and School Achievement," *Sociology of Education,* 37 (1954), pp. 271–78.

racial attitudes of children in kindergarten and first and second grades, Trager and Yarrow noted that their subjects frequently expressed open hostility toward blacks.[8] That negative racial attitudes increase as children grow older has been documented by Radke, Trager, and Davis.[9]

Because children come to school with negative racial attitudes, the school has some responsibility to help them develop and maintain more positive outlooks. This applies to both white and minority group children, for research suggests that children who have positive racial attitudes are more self-accepting.[10] Quillen states that ". . . the American school system is an expression of the American way of life. It developed to sustain the core values which the American people want to preserve and realize more fully."[11] Respect for others, regardless of race, creed, economic status, or national origin is a central tenet of the American democratic ideology. The school has a major responsibility to help children develop racial attitudes that are consistent with democratic ideals.

TEXTBOOKS AND RACIAL ATTITUDES

Some studies suggest that textbooks contribute to the negative evaluations that children typically express toward Negroes. After a study of textbooks used in the public schools, Black wrote:

> Among the perversions committed in the name of education, few equal the schoolbook's treatment of the Negro and his history. For more than 150 years he was presented to millions of children, both black and white, as a sub-human, incapable of achieving culture, happy in servitude, a passive outsider in the development and struggles of the American peoples.[12]

Since the 1940's, there have been a number of studies concerned with the image of the Negro in textbooks. Most of these studies sup-

[8]Helen G. Trager and Marian R. Yarrow, *They Learn What They Live* (New York: Harper & Row, 1952), pp. 140, 155.

[9]Marian Radke, Helen G. Trager, and Hadassah Davis, "Social Perceptions and Attitudes of Children," *Genetic Psychology Monographs*, 40 (November 1959), p. 440.

[10]R. Trent, "The Correlates of Self-acceptance Among Negro Children," Unpublished doctoral dissertation, Teachers College, Columbia University, New York, 1953.

[11]James Quillen, "The Evolving Objectives of Education in American Life," *The Educational Record*, 39 (July 1958), p. 222.

[12]Hillel Black, *The American Schoolbook* (New York: William Morrow, 1967), p. 106.

port the opinions expressed by Black. A study reported in 1949 by the American Council on Education indicated that authors largely avoided discussion of the Negro.[13] When he was discussed, it was within the context of slavery and Reconstruction, and he was portrayed as a jubilant Sambo who had freedom thrust upon him by benevolent Lincoln. Textbooks also suggested that Nat Turner, Gabriel Prosser, and other leaders of slave rebellions were fanatics, that stupid blacks and radical Northern Republicans corruptly ruled the South during Reconstruction, and that the Ku Klux Klan emerged as a response to corrupt rule by blacks, scalawags, and carpetbaggers.[13] In 1961, Marcus replicated the study of the American Council on Education.[14] He found that the image of the black man in textbooks had not substantially changed since 1949. Marcus also noted that very little was found in textbooks about the black man's attempts to resist discrimination, and that America was portrayed as a lily-white society.

Kenneth M. Stampp and a committee of historians analyzed the treatment of the Negro in the American history textbooks most frequently used in California.[15] Like the other researchers, they concluded that textbooks often omit discussion of the Negro and race relations. This committee reported that textbooks emphasized the harmonious aspects of race relations in our nation and largely ignored the long history of violence between blacks and whites. They also noted that textbooks frequently justify discrimination and racial prejudice.

A number of other studies of minority groups in textbooks have confirmed the findings by the American Council on Education, Marcus, and the Stampp Committee. In 1964, Golden found that very little information was presented about minority and ethnic groups in primary social studies textbooks.[16] In 1966, Anderson[17] studied fourteen elementary social studies textbooks and concluded that they failed to

---

[13]The Committee on the Study of Teaching Materials in Intergroup Relations, *Intergroup Relations in Teaching Materials* (Washington, D.C.: American Council on Education, 1949), p. 10.

[14]Lloyd Marcus, *The Treatment of Minorities in Secondary School Textbooks* (New York: Anti-Defamation League of B'nai B'rith, 1962), pp. 8–9, 48.

[15]Kenneth M. Stampp *et al.,* "The Negro in American History Textbooks," Mimeographed Report, California Department of Public Instruction, pp. 1–22.

[16]Loretta Golden, "The Treatment of Minority Groups in Primary Social Studies Textbooks," Unpublished Ed.D. dissertation, Stanford University, 1964.

[17]Astrid C. Anderson, "The Treatment of Racial and Cultural Diversity in Elementary Social Studies Textbooks" (mimeographed report), Medford, Mass.: The Lincoln Filene Center for Citizenship and Public Affairs, Tufts University, 1966, pp. 16–27.

help youngsters develop understandings and concepts that are essential to an effective program in intergroup education. Sloan studied the treatment of the Negro in thirteen modern secondary American history textbooks.[18] Although his findings mainly confirm those of the earlier researchers, he concluded that the Negro is more fairly represented in more recent books.

The most comprehensive study since that of the American Council on Education in 1949 is the one conducted by this writer, in which a technique called thematic analysis was used to analyze the treatment of the Negro in a sample of thirty-six elementary American history textbooks. I found that textbooks do not frequently describe racial violence and conflict. However, authors describe racial violence as frequently as they describe peaceful and friendly relations between blacks and whites. Authors emphasize the achievements of individual black heroes rather than the condition of the majority of black people in the nation. Negroes are discussed more frequently in books published in 1968 than in books published in 1964.

These studies indicate that the treatment of the Negro in textbooks is improving, but the subject is still largely neglected in most of the books used in the public school. This is an immensely important fact since most of the school's curriculum is built around the textbook and because recent research supports the idea that teaching materials *do* affect children's racial attitudes.

Litcher and Johnson studied the racial attitudes of second grade white children after one group had used multiethnic readers and the other group had used "all-white" readers. The authors found that the children who had used the multiethnic readers expressed more positive racial attitudes than the group that used all-white readers. The authors wrote, "Use of the multi-ethnic readers resulted in marked positive change in the subjects' attitudes toward Negroes."[19] Trager and Yarrow found that children who were exposed to a curriculum that emphasized the positive attributes of minority groups expressed racial attitudes that were more positive after the experience than before it.[20]

Johnson investigated the effects of a black history course on the racial attitudes of a group of Negro children. He concluded that the

---

[18]Irving Sloan, *The Negro in Modern History Textbooks* (Chicago: American Federation of Teachers, AFL-CIO, 1966), p. 7.

[19]John H. Litcher and David W. Johnson, "Changes in Attitudes of White Elementary School Students After Use of Multi-Ethnic Readers," *Journal of Educational Psychology,* 60 (1969), pp. 148–52.

[20]Trager and Yarrow, *op. cit.* pp. 231–36.

course had a positive effect on the children's racial attitudes and self-concepts. He wrote:

> ... they become more confident in themselves, more convinced that Negroes and whites are equal, and more militant toward civil rights. The findings of the study ... can be taken as tentative evidence that ... [the teaching of] Negro history and culture can be effective in raising Negro boys' attitudes toward self and toward Negroes.[21]

As these studies indicate, teaching materials and methods affect youngsters' racial attitudes and self-concepts. It is therefore imperative that the school plan and execute a systematic program in intergroup education with the aim of minimizing racial conflict and racial polarization.

THE TEACHER'S ROLE IN INTERGROUP EDUCATION

It is important to have multiethnic and multiracial teaching materials in an effective program in intergroup education, but the attitudes, perceptions, and predispositions of the classroom teacher are much more important than the materials he uses. Cuban notes:

> Less attention should be paid to additional books and courses ... and more to the craftsman who will use the tools. Preachers of Black History know that the person is far more important than the materials he uses.[22]

Before the teacher can plan and execute a successful program in intergroup education he must clarify his own attitudes toward minority groups. Joyce commented:

> Over the years we have subscribed to the time-honored principle that teaching materials are only as good as the teachers using them. This principle, coupled with the inescapable fact that educators, like most other Americans, are likely to harbor negative attitudes toward racial and ethnic minorities, suggests that before the classroom teacher can present his pupils with the accurate, realistic image of minority group relations that is so desperately needed, he will need to re-examine, clarify, and modify his own attitudes and predispositions toward minorities.[23]

[21]David W. Johnson, "Freedom School Effectiveness: Changes in Attitudes of Negro Children," *The Journal of Applied Behavioral Science*, 2 (1966), pp. 325–30.
[22]Larry Cuban, "Black History, Negro History, and White Folk," *Saturday Review* (September 21, 1968), p. 65.
[23]William W. Joyce, "Minority Groups in American Society: Imperatives for Educators," *Social Education*, 33 (April 1969), p. 433.

Much research indicates that teachers typically have negative attitudes toward poor and black children. Gottlieb found that white teachers describe Negro pupils as talkative, lazy, fun-loving, high-strung, and rebellious.[24] It is imperative that teachers develop more positive attitudes toward black people and their culture if they are to play effective roles in helping youngsters develop positive attitudes and self-images. This is true because children can accurately perceive the teacher's attitudes, and because teachers are "significant others" to the children they teach. In our society we acquire identity from other human beings who are "significant" to us and incorporate it within ourselves. We validate our identity through the evaluations of those who are influential in our lives. A study by Davidson and Lang indicates that the assessment a child makes of himself is related to the assessment "significant people" make of him. The study showed that a pupil's self-appraisal is significantly related to his perceptions of his teacher's feelings.[25]

Teachers who have positive attitudes toward minority groups, who accurately perceive the role of the black man in our history, and who are convinced of the need for a multiethnic and multiracial curriculum, will be less inclined to tolerate textbooks that perpetuate misconceptions, and will supplement the textbook when it has serious gaps. A section of the next chapter suggests some strategies that teachers may use to clarify their racial attitudes. Whether the social studies curriculum becomes truly multiethnic and multiracial will ultimately depend on the intent and resourcefulness of the classroom teacher, regardless of the recent improvements in teaching materials.

THE INQUIRY APPROACH TO THE STUDY OF RACE RELATIONS

Although children should master facts, concepts, and social science generalizations, the main goal of social education should be to equip pupils with strategies for solving the social problems in tomorrow's world. We can best help students to become adept in solving social problems by approaching the study of social issues scientifically. However, students must be *concerned* about problems in order to

[24]David Gottlieb, "Teaching and Students: The Views of Negro and White Teachers," *Sociology of Education*, 27 (1964), pp. 245–53.

[25]Helen H. Davidson and Gerhard Lang, "Children's Perceptions of Teachers'. Feelings Toward Them Related to Self-perception, School Achievement and Behavior," *Journal of Experimental Education*, 29 (1960), pp. 107–18.

feel that they merit study. Racial issues stimulate concern and reflection because they force students to examine their value beliefs.[26]

In utilizing an inquiry approach in studying race relations, children will identify problems, formulate hypotheses, collect data, evaluate evidence in terms of credence and relevance, and draw conclusions related to the hypotheses the class has formulated. Massialas and Cox list several factors that distinguish the inquiring classroom from the traditional classroom. In an inquiring classroom there is an ". . . open psychological climate of discussion, the use of hypotheses in directing discussions, and [an] emphasis on the use of reliable evidence in relation to these hypotheses."[27]

For example, when the class studies the civil rights movement, the students may pose the question, "What is black power?" They may then state their notions about the meanings of this concept. In collecting, analyzing, and evaluating evidence—which may be in the form of statements by W. E. B. DuBois, Malcolm X, Stokley Carmichael, H. Rap Brown, Paul Harvey, and Lester Maddox—they may find themselves rejecting many of their earlier notions about black power. Each student should be encouraged to reach his independent conclusions, and be able to defend them and to examine the methods and assumptions from which they arose. If a student reaches an unlikely conclusion, the most we can do is to encourage him to begin his inquiry anew, for the ultimate goal of social education is to help students develop a commitment to inquiry, and not to make them unthinking consumers of conclusions derived by others.[28] Throughout this book, the author suggests strategies to stimulate students to inquire into racial problems.

CONCLUSION

If we are to mitigate racial tension, invoke a deserved respect for the black American, create democratic racial attitudes, and contribute to the assimilation of the Negro into the mainstream of American life, we must expose all children to the contributions that the Negro has made to American life and to the problems he still faces.

[26]Maurice P. Hunt and Lawrence E. Metcalf, *Teaching High School Social Studies* (New York: Harper & Row, 1955) pp. 431–53.
[27]Byron G. Massialas and C. Benjamin Cox, *Inquiry in Social Studies* (New York: McGraw-Hill, 1966), p. 112.
[28]James A. Banks, "Varieties of History: Negro, Black, White," *Harvard Educational Review*, 39 (Winter 1969), pp. 155–58.

2

Organizing and Planning Instruction

ORGANIZING INSTRUCTION IN THE ELEMENTARY GRADES

The black experience in America can be presented as a separate unit or it can be treated within the context of a regular history or social studies unit. Ideally, the role of the Negro in America should be studied within the total context of American history. For example, when studying about the discovery of America, students can be introduced to Pedro Alonzo Niño, a black man who was the navigator of one of Columbus' ships. Students should also learn about the black men who were with the early Spanish explorers in the New World, such as the thirty black men who were with Balboa when he discovered the Pacific Ocean and those who were with Cortez when he conquered the Aztecs of Mexico. They will be intrigued by interesting black men such as Estavancio who was the first man, except for the native Indians, to travel through the southwestern part of the United States. During a study of the Revolutionary period, famous Negroes of the time, such as Benjamin Banneker, the mathematician and inventor, and Phillis Wheatley, the poet, should be included. There are numerous opportunities to incorporate materials on the Negro into the total context of the regular social studies units.

Although a *totally integrated* approach to the study of the black American is in many respects ideal, one comprehensive unit on the black American in the elementary grades may be necessary to help children dispel misconceptions and fully appreciate the outstanding contributions that blacks have made to American life. Children, both white and nonwhite, are likely to have many erroneous notions about the black man's role in the making of America. A major reason for this is that social studies textbooks have largely ignored the black man. Although a special and concentrated unit in one of the elementary grades can be effective, it must be both *preceded* and *followed* by lessons on the black experience integrated into the *total* school curriculum.

Because our era is characterized by much racial tension and strife, children should be helped to understand these problems in order that their environment will be more meaningful to them and so that, as adults, they will be better prepared to help ameliorate racial problems and tension. Unless they are sufficiently aware of racial problems and of sound approaches to solving them, they will be unable to make effective contributions to the mitigation of racial tension and conflict. Because children, both white and black, frequently have negative racial attitudes toward Negroes, a comprehensive unit on the black American will hopefully help to develop healthy racial attitudes in both black and white students and will also help Negro pupils develop healthier self-concepts.

Recent research conducted by the author suggests that middle grade pupils have erroneous notions about the social problems of the poor, the nature of slums, and the causes of violent racial outbreaks in urban areas. Also, the students had very little knowledge of outstanding black Americans who have made significant contributions to American life. Because violent outbreaks do occur in our cities, children should be helped to understand the nature of racial violence and conflict. They should be exposed to a social studies curriculum that is consistent with their world and their needs. When there is a lag between reality and the social studies curriculum, the school becomes meaningless to many children from all racial and ethnic groups. The black experience should be given special emphasis at some point during the elementary grades to make the social studies more congruent with reality, to compensate for the many misconceptions that children have about blacks, to make up for the deficits in basal textbooks, and to counteract the negative evaluations of the black American which children have acquired in the larger society and which they bring to school. *The unique problems of the black American warrant special attention.* A thorough and comprehensive unit, reinforced by lessons on the black experience throughout the elementary school years, is probably the most effective plan of instruction.

If a major unit on the black American is taught in the fifth grade, pupils in all the other grades should also be exposed to materials on the black experience in an integrated fashion. For example, in kindergarten, when children are learning about community helpers, they should be made aware of the fact that many community helpers are black. Although this may not be true in every community, it is true in many of our metropolitan areas. If children do not learn about black policemen, postmen, and firemen, they are likely to assume, as many children have, that all community helpers are white. If a considerable proportion of the residents in the community are Negro and there are no black community helpers in the community, the teacher may ask the children to speculate why. This would be a tremendous opportunity to begin developing children's inquiry skills.

The teacher should not be reluctant to mention racial issues in kindergarten for fear that he will unnecessarily focus the children's attention on racial matters. Research evidence indicates that children are aware of race and racial significance long before they enter school. Thus, it is our responsibility as educators to help them critically examine the racial situation around them, clarify and examine their own racial attitudes, and help them develop more positive predispositions and perceptions.

We noted that in planning for sequence, a special unit in the fifth grade should be *preceded* by learning experiences related to the Negro and race relations. The special unit should also be *followed* by learning activities related to the Negro throughout the elementary years. These activities should not be limited to social studies but should be pursued in other subject areas as well. When the class studies twentieth-century literature, the children should be introduced to the poetry of the Pulitzer Prize winning poet Gwendolyn Brooks. In science, they should learn about the contributions of Percy Julian and Charles Drew. Blacks such as Marian Anderson and Henry O. Tanner can be presented during the fine arts period.

In summary, it is desirable to expose students to a special unit on the black American to attempt to dispel many of their misconceptions and to help them understand the racial strife in our era. But it is also essential that pupils be exposed to meaningful learning experiences related to the black American throughout the elementary and high school years and that the material be integrated into the total school curriculum. Such an ambitious program in intergroup relations will be challenging, and it will be equally rewarding to both students and teachers. Students are usually amazed to discover the tremendous role the black man has played in the building of America.

CLARIFYING LONG-RANGE INSTRUCTIONAL GOALS

Although this book is mainly concerned with the *how* of teaching the black experience, rather than the *why*, it is essential that the classroom teacher have a clear idea of what he is trying to accomplish in order for him to plan meaningful learning experiences for his pupils. The teacher should know the long-range objectives of his instructional program.

Different teachers have different instructional goals, and will there- fore use their materials in different ways. The kinds of evaluation exercises a teacher plans for a unit illuminates the objectives he has formulated. For example, Mrs. Jones might plan an evaluation exer- cise at the end of her unit on the civil rights movement that requires the students to list the leaders of the movement and the names of cities where large civil rights demonstrations took place. Mr. Lee, in giving a test at the end of his unit on the same subject, might ask the pupils to discuss the word "resistance" and to illustrate an under- standing of the word by citing instances of resistance that were examined during the unit. Mrs. Wright might test for a slightly different kind of understanding. She might ask her students to list, in sentence form, the conditions that lead to "social oppression" and to discuss the kinds of reactions that victims of oppression usually evidence. A fourth teacher, Mr. Clay, might test his pupils by giving them a case study of a Negro couple who have just moved into a white neighborhood and are faced with the hostility of their neigh- bors. This teacher may ask his students to (1) identify the problem in the situation, (2) collect and analyze data related to the problem, (3) pose possible solutions to the problem, and (4) indicate the possible consequences of the proposed solutions and the values and assumptions from which they originated.

The teachers in these hypothetical situations have different long- range instructional objectives for their units. Mrs. Jones is mainly concerned that her pupils master specific *facts* about the civil rights movement, such as the names of key leaders and cities. Mr. Lee believes that his students should develop an understanding of *con- cepts* or main ideas, such as the concept of "resistance." Mrs. Wright is more interested in helping her pupils derive *generalizations* or "broad inclusive statements" about social science. Mr. Clay believes that students should develop inquiry skills and learn to identify problems, state them clearly, formulate hypotheses, gather data, and reach valid conclusions that can guide action.

Actually, these understandings and skills are not mutually exclusive, but a teacher might emphasize one type of understanding or skill development and de-emphasize others. Many teachers who are primarily concerned that their students master facts often do not attempt to help them attain higher level understandings. However, a teacher cannot help his pupils master concepts, generalizations, and inquiry skills without the use of facts. *Facts* are specific statements that refer to limited phenomena, such as "Martin Luther King led the Montgomery March," and "Rosa Parks refused to give up her seat on the bus to a white man." A *concept* is a word or phrase with generalized and diverse meanings, such as "resistance," "violence," and "prejudice." Many facts can be classified under one broad concept. Womack defines a *generalization* as ". . . a broad inclusive statement in complete grammatical sentence form which serves as a principle or rule for the social studies."[1] Some examples are: "Social conflict leads to social change under certain conditions," and "All human beings live in groups." Note that generalizations are made up of concepts. Sometimes a generalization is defined as a statement that shows the relationship between concepts. "Conflict," "change," and "groups" are among the concepts that make up the generalizations in our examples. Thus, if youngsters are to master social science generalizations, they must first grasp facts and concepts.

According to Jarolimek, facts, concepts, and generalizations are kinds of *understandings*, but the ability to inquire and solve social problems are types of *skills*.[2] However, a student may derive generalizations by utilizing an inquiry process. Inquiry usually involves identifying a problem, stating the problem in precise terms, gathering data related to the problem, and reaching tentative conclusions. A class that is studying the problem, "What is black power?" may derive several generalizations regarding social power, such as "Every ethnic group develops a unique form of power," and "Power is needed to bring about social change."

Before a teacher can formulate and execute meaningful learning

---

[1]James G. Womack, *Discovering the Structure of Social Studies* (New York: Benziger Brothers, 1966), p. 2.

[2]John Jarolimek, *Social Studies in Elementary Education* (New York: Macmillan, 1967), p. 57.

experiences in race relations, he needs to differentiate between *facts, concepts, generalizations,* and *inquiry skills.* Then he must determine which understandings and skills he will give the greatest emphasis. One of the basic assumptions of this book is that social studies education should help youngsters master concepts, derive generalizations, and become proficient in dealing with social problems. Therefore, many examples will illustrate how these understandings and skills can be developed during a study of the black experience in the elementary and high school grades.

Students must have a command of facts before they can master concepts and generalizations and handle social problems. Too frequently, however, we do not help youngsters progress beyond the mastery of facts. It is difficult to justify requiring youngsters to master facts unless they are used to help them learn to deal with social problems more skillfully. The ultimate goal of social education should be to help the adults of tomorrow solve the problems that will confront them.

In addition to ascertaining the kinds of understandings and skills that he wishes his pupils to master, the teacher should also determine the *attitudes* he wants his pupils to develop. A discussion of attitude modification in intergroup education is presented later in this chapter.

FORMULATING SPECIFIC INSTRUCTIONAL OBJECTIVES

No meaningful, effective learning experiences can take place unless the teacher has clearly in mind the outcomes he wishes his pupils to evidence at the conclusion of a unit. Without effective objectives, the teacher will be unable to ascertain whether his unit has been effective. According to Mager, "... a meaningfully stated objective is one that succeeds in communicating to the reader the writer's instructional intent ... [it] ... excludes the greatest number of possible alternatives to [a] goal."[3] If an objective is carefully stated, any teacher should be able to use it to guide pupils toward the exact goal that the writer of the objective intends. Thus, if you state that your instructional goal is for the pupils to *understand* the role of the Negro in America, it is possible that another teacher who reads your objective would interpret the word "understand" in a different way than

[3] Robert F. Mager, *Preparing Instructional Objectives* (Palo Alto: Fearon Publishers, 1962), p. 10.

you had intended. Although "understanding" is a desirable goal, it is difficult to evaluate and it must be defined behaviorally. It is best to state objectives in such a way that their outcomes can be readily assessed. To determine whether children understand the role of the black man in American society, we must behaviorally define the word "understand." We may be willing to say that a pupil understands the role of the Negro in America if he is able to *list* the most important contributions the Negro has made to American life, to *construct* a chart showing these contributions, to *compare* these contributions with those of other ethnic groups, and to identify the contributions on a multiple-choice test. We may behaviorally define *understand* in other ways. A student who is able to write ten generalizations regarding the Negro's role in American history, or to identify the most important concepts related to the black experience in America, demonstrates higher level understandings. In formulating objectives, it is necessary to identify the *terminal behavior* we wish the learner to evidence at the end of the learning experience.[4]

Other examples may further clarify the problem of stating meaningful objectives in behavioral terms. One of your major objectives in a unit on the Negro may be that students should "grasp the significance" of black slavery in the United States. Once you have stated this broad, general objective, you must describe the kind of terminal behavior you will accept as evidence that the student has "grasped the significance of slavery." Your behavioral objective may be similar to the one below:

To Grasp the Significance of Black Slavery in the United States

Behavior:

1. The student should be able to *list* the kinds of work that slaves performed.

2. The student should be able to identify the leaders of three slave rebellions.

3. The student should be able to *compare* and *contrast* slavery in the New England colonies with slavery in the Southern and Middle Colonies.

4. The student should be able to write five generalizations about black slavery in the United States.

Once the terminal behavior has been clearly delineated, the *conditions* under which the learner will be expected to perform and the

[4]*Ibid.*, p. 12.

level of acceptable performance should be formulated.[5] Looking at our example, the teacher must determine whether the student will be allowed to use the text when he is asked to "list the kinds of work the slaves performed" or whether he will have to accomplish this educational task without external aids. The teacher must also determine whether the student will be required to list *every* kind of work the slaves did or only some kinds of work.

One of the central objectives of any social studies experience should be to help children develop and strengthen their inquiry and problem-solving skills. Again, the teacher must define the kinds of terminal behavior he will accept as evidence of the ability to *inquire*. One skill objective during a study of slavery in the United States might be that "The student should be able to *inquire* into problems related to slavery." In attempting to *state* this objective in behavioral terms, we may derive the following more specific goals: The student should be able to read contemporary accounts of slavery and *identify:* (1) the problem discussed by the writer, (2) the writer's basic assumptions and values, (3) the writer's biases, (4) the writer's reason(s) for writing the document, (5) the audience the writer had in mind, and (6) the writer's conclusions.

The teacher can think of other ways to define *inquiry* behaviorally. The student may be required to identify the problem in a movie, a story, or in a role-playing situation. After recognizing a problem in a role-playing situation, the student might be required to pose possible solutions to the problem, and to predict the possible consequences of alternative solutions. When stating alternatives, the student should also be required to state his assumptions and the criteria used in deriving alternatives.[6]

In formulating objectives regarding inquiry skills, some attempt should be made to state learning conditions and levels of acceptable performance. When a learner is required to identify a writer's basic assumptions, values, biases, and conclusions, he may or may not be permitted to ask the teacher leading questions, he may be required to work independently of other pupils, or he may only be permitted to use the document he is analyzing as a reference. Formulating acceptable levels of performance when stating inquiry objectives poses certain difficulties since student responses are likely to be less

[5]*Ibid.*
[6]Bernice Goldmark, *Social Studies: A Method of Inquiry* (Belmont, Cal.: Wadsworth Publishing Company, 1968), pp. 149–54.

standardized and more individualized in inquiry learning situations. For example, if two students read the same document, each of them may think that it deals with a different problem, and each may have defensible reasons for his choice of problem statement. Although difficulties are inherent, some attempt should be made to formulate criteria for acceptable performance. If a student is required to identify a problem in a document, a movie, or a role-playing situation, acceptable criteria may include: (1) stating the *major* problem rather than any subordinate problems, (2) stating the problem clearly and precisely, (3) stating the problem in one complete sentence, and (4) stating reasons for problem choice.

FORMULATING AFFECTIVE OBJECTIVES

In addition to formulating *cognitive* instructional objectives (such as the ability to identify a problem), we are also concerned with objectives in the *affective domain*—that is, we are interested in modifying children's racial attitudes toward the black American and helping them to appreciate the contributions the Negro has made to American life. Formulating objectives in the affective domain and establishing acceptable performance levels for such objectives is a challenging task. Some suggestions are apropos. The teacher may note the children's verbal comments about Negroes before and after a unit or lessons on the black experience. If the class is racially mixed, he may observe the children's social interaction patterns before and after the unit in order to ascertain whether positive change in racial attitudes has occurred during the unit.

The teacher can formalize this procedure by carrying out a simple action research project. He can design a simple racial attitude scale and administer it before and after the unit to determine if there has been a change in the students' expressed racial attitudes. One objective of the unit could be: "The students will express more positive attitudes toward Negroes after the unit than before the unit on a racial attitude inventory." Thus, the teacher could easily determine whether or not this objective had been attained and to what extent. Many racial inventories are available for use with adults. It may be necessary for the teacher to modify these inventories before he uses any of them with his class. The following is a section of a racial attitude scale developed by this author for use with fifth grade urban children:

Directions to Pupils: Check only those words or phrases that describe *most* Negroes.

____ work hard to get ahead	____ often loud
____ speak clearly	____ good in sports
____ like to fight a lot	____ good in different subjects
____ work well with others	____ good in music
____ creative	____ lazy
____ moody	____ happy
____ mad at the world	____ bright
____ dull	____ cute

Check only those words or phrases that describe *most* whites.

____ work hard to get ahead	____ often loud
____ speak clearly	____ good in sports
____ like to fight a lot	____ good in different subjects
____ work well with others	____ good in music
____ creative	____ lazy
____ moody	____ happy
____ mad at the world	____ bright
____ dull	____ cute

This inventory has parallel check lists so that the teacher can compare the way children think of blacks in comparison to whites. The child who checks "like to fight a lot" under the "Negro" category, for example, may think that *all* people "like to fight a lot." When we compare the pupil's responses on each check list, we can determine which characteristics he attributes to all people and which to Negroes and to whites. It might be a good idea to administer the two parts of the inventory at different times so that the possibility of responses on one part of the inventory influencing responses on the other part would be considerably lessened. This list of descriptive words and phrases could be extended or shortened, depending upon the teaching situation and upon how much information the teacher desires about the children's racial attitudes. In any case, positive, negative, and neutral items should be randomly distributed in the inventory in order to increase the validity of the responses.

There are also other kinds of racial attitude inventories that the teacher may construct or obtain. Several types of inventories were constructed by Dr. John S. Gibson and his associates at the Lincoln Filene Center for Citizenship and Public Affairs during their development of a program in intergroup education for the elementary grades. One is called a Sentence Completion Instrument.[7] In it the

---

[7]John S. Gibson, *The Intergroup Relations Curriculum: A Program for Elementary School Education* (Vol. I) (Medford, Mass.: The Lincoln Filene Center for Citizenship and Public Affairs, Tufts University, 1969), pp. 141a–141f.

student is asked to complete statements about ethnic groups, such as "Most Negroes_____," and "Most American Indians_____." In Part II of this inventory, the student is given a long list of adjectival phrases and asked to use them to complete statements about various racial and ethnic groups.

By comparing the responses before and after the unit, the teacher can determine if it has been effective in modifying pupils' expressed racial attitudes. In order to assess the *stability* of change in expressed racial attitudes, the teacher could administer inventories immediately after the unit and again two or three months later. Changes in attitudes are not always maintained over time.

The teacher may also devise a number of other techniques to ascertain youngsters' racial attitudes. A third grade teacher in the Tacoma, Washington, public schools asked her pupils to write anonymous "Opinion Papers" in which they gave their opinions of Negroes before and after they undertook a unit on the black American.[8] The following statements are some of the opinions expressed by the pupils during the initial stage of the unit:

> They have greasy hands and skin.
> Their babies are born white and turn black.
> They eat different food.
> They are dirty.
> They are mean. (Many references to riots)
> Their parents don't like to sit by them.

Among the opinions that the students expressed after they had taken the unit are these:

> Negroes are the same as us and have the same feelings.
> If we tell our parents about famous Negroes maybe they will like them better.
> If a white man and a Negro apply for a job why does the white man usually get it?
> We must change laws so everyone is equal.

As the opinions expressed by this class of all-white third graders indicate, youngsters typically come to school with many negative racial attitudes and misconceptions. Through a well-formulated and executed program in intergroup education, such attitudes can be modified and misconceptions can be corrected, as was done in the course of this effective unit.

---

[8]*The History of Negro Life in America* (Tacoma, Wash.: Tacoma Public Schools, 1968), pp. 43–44. Used with permission.

RACIAL INVENTORIES IN THE PRIMARY GRADES

The kindergarten or primary grade teacher often will not be able to use attitude inventories that require pupils to read and write for the simple reason that many children in these grades do not possess these skills. However, the teacher may use other techniques to ascertain pupil racial attitudes. The kindergarten teacher may use the method utilized by Morland in his study of the racial attitudes of Negro and white kindergarteners, in which he showed them pictures of black and white children and asked them which children they would prefer for playmates. By keeping a record of the preferences expressed by the children, the teacher could construct a profile of his students' racial attitudes. The teacher may also obtain a collection of black and white dolls, and try to determine which types of dolls the pupils prefer most frequently. A formal but simplified interview may also be used to determine the racial attitudes of kindergarten and primary grade children. The teacher may begin by saying, "Most Negroes _____," and ask the student to complete the sentence. The child could be asked to respond to similar statements about other racial and ethnic minorities.

IMPROVING THE SELF-CONCEPT

Research cited in Chapter 1 indicates that black children often have low and deflated self-concepts. Some research also indicates that children who are more accepting of others are also more accepting of themselves. Thus, a fruitful objective of a unit on the Negro is to help both black and white children develop more positive self-images. A teacher can ascertain whether or not this goal has been attained by administering a self-concept scale before and after a unit on the black experience in America. There are a number of self-concept scales already available for use with children.[9] The teacher may wish to construct his own scale, but there are some advantages to using a scale that has already been standardized. Such a scale is likely to be more reliable and valid than an untested one.

One useful scale is the Piers-Harris Measure of Self-concept Inventory. This scale attempts to ascertain "global" or generic self-concept. It has been widely used and standardized, and both the standardization data and the instrument may be obtained by the teacher.

[9]For descriptions of self-concept inventories see Ruth Wylie, *The Self-concept* (Lincoln: University of Nebraska Press, 1961), p. 86ff.

The inventory includes eighty items. The teacher could use the entire instrument or a modified form of it. Sample items from this inventory follow:

The Way I Feel About Myself[10]

Directions to Pupils: Here are a set of statements. Some of them are true of you and so you will circle the YES. Some are not true of you and so you will circle the NO. Answer every question even if some are hard to decide. There are no right or wrong answers. Only you can tell how you feel about yourself, so we hope you will mark the way you really feel inside.

1.	My classmates make fun of me.	Yes	No
2.	I am a happy person.	Yes	No
3.	It is hard for me to make friends.	Yes	No
4.	I am often sad.	Yes	No

The Piers-Harris inventory measures a global or general type of self-concept (including anxiety, academic status, popularity, and physical appearance).

Brookover and his associates maintain that there are many different kinds of self-concepts that we can delineate.[11] They have developed a scale to measure the "self-concept of ability." This instrument requires the student to indicate his perceptions of his ability to achieve in school and in later years. Brookover's research indicates that a high self-concept of ability is a *necessary* condition, but not a *sufficient* one for high academic achievement. In other words, students with high self-concepts of ability may or may not achieve highly, but few if any students with low self-concepts of ability will ever achieve at high levels.

It is hypothesized that black children have lower self-concepts than white children because of the negative evaluations of Negroes that our society often makes. Thus, a unit on the black experience that illuminates the positives of the Negro race should increase the Negro child's self-concept. Since children who are more accepting of others are also more self-accepting, white children who are exposed

[10]Ellen V. Piers and Dale B. Harris, "The Piers-Harris Children's Self-concept Scale (The Way I Feel About Myself)," (Nashville, Tenn.: Counselor Recordings and Tests, 1969). Copyright © 1969 by Ellen V. Piers and Dale B. Harris. Used with permission. Discussed in Ellen V. Piers and Dale B. Harris, "Age and Other Correlates of Self-concept in Children," *Journal of Educational Psychology,* 55 (April 1964), pp. 91–95.

[11]Wilbur H. Brookover, Ann Paterson, and Shailer Thomas, "Self-concept of Ability and School Achievement," *Sociology of Education,* 37 (1964), pp. 271–78.

to such a unit may also develop more positive racial attitudes and therefore more positive self-concepts. Of course, children who express few if any negative racial attitudes at the beginning of the unit should not be expected to experience a significant gain in self-concept. Since a high self-concept is related to high academic achievement, a higher self-concept may therefore result in higher academic achievement. Thus, the teacher might want to see if his pupils, especially the black children, experience a gain in achievement after a unit on the black experience in America.

THE SOCIOGRAM

If a class is racially mixed, the teacher has a unique opportunity to utilize the sociogram to determine if there has been a change in the pupils' social interactions after a unit on the black experience. Although a racial attitude inventory can assess expressed attitudes, social interaction patterns of youngsters represent a more valid indication of their true attitudes. If more white children choose Negroes as pals (and vice versa) after the unit than before, and especially if these relationships endure over time, the teacher can justifiably conclude that the unit had positive effects on the children's racial attitudes and behavior.[12]

EVALUATING LEARNING OUTCOMES

If the learning objectives have been stated in behavioral terms with desired outcomes specified, evaluation will be greatly facilitated. In addition to stating objectives in behavioral terms, the teacher must state some minimum level of acceptable performance. Thus, if the students are required to list the leaders of the slave revolts, the teacher must indicate whether the listing of two of the leaders or all of them will be required as an indication of satisfactory performance. The evaluation can be no better than the objectives stated at the beginning of the unit. It is all too easy for the teacher to lose sight of the central objectives of the unit and terminate evaluation activities by testing the pupils on content that is peripheral to the major intended outcomes. The major outcomes may be the mastery of *facts, concepts, generalizations,* or *inquiry skills,* or a combination of these understandings and skills.

[12]For a useful guide to various data-gathering inventories for use with elementary pupils, see R. Fox, M. B. Luszki, and R. Schmuck, *Diagnosing Classroom Learning Environments* (Chicago: Science Research Associates, 1966).

Suggestions have already been given as to how the teacher can ascertain achievement in the affective domain. These suggested methods, as well as methods that the teacher may devise himself, are useful in ascertaining learning in this difficult area. By casual observation of the students' verbal and other behavior, the teacher will be able to assess important learning outcomes in the affective domain of attitudes and appreciations. Whenever possible, these observations should be formalized and quantified. Formalization and quantification will strengthen and facilitate evaluation procedures.

In evaluating learning outcomes in the *cognitive domain* (the mastery of understandings and skills), it is useful to administer a test on the black experience and problems in race relations before and after the unit. One such test has been developed by John Georgeoff of Purdue University. This test of *facts* on the black experience has been used with hundreds of children in the Gary, Indiana, Public Schools. Often the teacher may wish to develop a test based on his own unit objectives. He may be primarily interested in testing mastery of facts, knowledge of concepts and generalizations, or the ability to inquire into racial problems. The examination of a test already developed, however, may give the teacher some useful ideas he can use in constructing his own test.

In planning and executing units or lessons on the black experience, the teacher must formulate meaningful behavioral objectives and effective evaluation exercises. The pupils can and should participate in structuring objectives and in planning evaluation exercises, but the teacher must guide these efforts and bear the major responsibility for facilitating the children's acquisition of essential understandings and skills. Without effective objectives and evaluating techniques, lessons on race relations are unlikely to produce the desired outcomes.

SELECTING AND ORGANIZING CONTENT FOR INSTRUCTION

The organization of the content of a unit on black Americans will depend on several important factors. Some of the most important are the results that the teacher wishes to achieve, the grade level and reading abilities of the pupils, the pupils' interests, and their previous learning experiences. For lower grade children or retarded readers, a desirable way to approach the study of the black experience is by utilizing biographies as the main source of information. By studying the biographies of famous black persons, the students can learn much about the Negro's contributions to our culture, the progress that black people have made in American society, and the racial problems that we still must solve. A well-structured unit utilizing biographies as the main source of information can also help youngsters master important concepts and generalizations regarding the black experience in America, and improve their inquiry and problem-solving skills.

One effective biographical inquiry approach was used by the author with fourth grade urban children, many of whom were retarded readers. The class formulated this problem: "How did famous black people overcome racial barriers?" After the problem had been stated in clear, precise terms, the class then had to determine the forms of data they would use to help them solve it. They decided that stories of the lives of outstanding black Americans would help them solve their problem. The teacher found biographies of famous black Americans and rewrote them at a sufficiently low level of difficulty to accommodate the reading ability of the pupils. Each biography (one person was studied each day) given to the class included seat exercises written by the teacher. The children answered such questions as these: What barriers did this individual face? How did he overcome them? What do you think he would have become if he had faced no barriers? More barriers? How do the barriers that he faced compare with those overcome by other famous people that we have studied?

To help the pupils attain skills in asking higher level questions, they were asked *why*, in their opinions, these individuals were motivated to achieve highly. The pupils suggested that some individuals achieved to gain friends, material goods and comfort, power, and personal satisfaction. They also thought that some individuals achieved because they felt that everyone was expected to achieve in our society. Some children thought that many black people achieved exceptionally well in order to help shatter white America's traditional image of the black man.

In many instances the children were exposed to several different versions of an individual's life. In these cases they were asked such questions as: Which account do you think comes closest to the true story? Why do you think so? How can we tell which account is most nearly accurate? Why are there different accounts of the same person's life?

The use of different accounts of the same person's life was not intended to make the students cynical, but to help them gain an appreciation of the difficulties involved in establishing historical "accuracy" and to strengthen their problem-solving skills. Exposing our youngsters to diverse historical interpretations is one of the surest ways to develop the critically minded citizens needed to deal with the baffling problems in this increasingly polarized society.

Each day a photograph of the individual being studied was displayed on the bulletin board. At the end of the unit, the pictures of all the famous people who had been studied were displayed together. Other techniques to develop student interest were also used. For instance, when the class learned about the poet Gwendolyn Brooks, her book of poetry, *Bronzeville Boys and Girls,* was read along with her biography. When Duke Ellington, Aretha Franklin, and Marian Anderson were the subjects, the class listened to recordings of their music.

To culminate the unit, the class prepared a pageant and presented it to the school assembly. Each child chose an outstanding Negro whom he had studied in depth, and then dramatized a significant event in his life. The children also made a mural chronicling the roles of great black Americans in the building of America. They called their mural "They Showed the Way."

Another problem that can be formulated with the use of biographies as sources of information is "What contributions have blacks made to America?" The students could also develop some related questions, such as "What contributions have Negroes made to science, art, music, sports, politics, and other fields?" Another related question may be "What effects have these contributions had on American society?" A unit organized around this problem will help students see clearly that the black man has made major contributions to the culture of our country.

Although problems that require only the use of biographies for their investigation are suitable for younger children or for children who have had little experience with other forms of social science data, this approach is inadequate for more experienced pupils. More mature children should formulate social problems that are of major concern, and that require the use of data from all of the social science disciplines, including census data, historical documents, surveys, photographs, biographies, fiction, demographic data, voting data, newspapers, and magazines. A necessary characteristic of all problems selected for study is that they be relevant and of concern to the students. Otherwise, students will not become emotionally involved in them, and the opportunities for initiating successful inquiry exercises will be reduced. Unless the student is concerned about a problem, he will not feel a need to inquire about it.

Whenever possible, the teacher should allow his pupils to select problems that reflect their interests and concerns. When a class studies American slavery, for example, the pupils could formulate a problem that would involve the study of slavery and also reflect their present interests and concerns. For example, a class could formulate the question, "What are the historical roots of black power?" and study the revolts that occurred on the slave ships, the slave rebellions, and the Underground Railroad as early manifestations of black resistance to oppression.

PLANNING A READING PROGRAM FOR THE TEACHER

Before a teacher can guide pupils' learning experiences in any area of social knowledge, he must possess a rather sophisticated grasp of the content. He must be well acquainted with major concepts and generalizations in the area, conflicting interpretations (there are many regarding the black experience in America), and with the major sources of information. It is especially important that teachers be familiar with sources so that they can help the more highly motivated and interested students to explore various topics in depth. For example, some children may be fascinated with the role of the black troops in the Civil War. The teacher should be able to direct them to appropriate source materials. When students encounter conflicting interpretations, such as those concerning Lincoln's attitudes toward Negroes and slavery, the teacher should be able to point out primary source materials, such as Lincoln's letters and speeches, and other sources that present both positive and negative views of Lincoln. The students should be encouraged to derive their own independent conclusions.

The materials listed in the bibliography at the end of this book will help the teacher plan and carry out a reading program on the black experience in America. Many of these books are in inexpensive paperback editions. One of the most important books on the subject is *From Slavery to Freedom* by John Hope Franklin, professor of history at the University of Chicago. Since its first publication in 1947, it has been a standard text for courses in black history. It has been revised several times and is an indispensable source for the teacher who initiates a unit or lessons on the black experience. The more expensive books listed in the bibliography can be purchased by the school for its professional library or can be borrowed from the local public library.

PLANNING A READING PROGRAM FOR THE PUPILS

Because basal social studies texts do not include sufficient information on the black experience in America, the teacher must formulate a reading program for the pupils. This program should not only include factual books about Africa and American Negroes, but should include African and American Negro folklore, biographies, and fiction. The unit or lesson should reflect all of the learning areas, such as fine arts, language arts, writing, and whenever possible, mathematics. When students are studying slavery, they should read biographies such as the Newbery Award winners *I, Juan de Pareja* by Elizabeth B. De Trevino and *Amos Fortune: Free Man* by Elizabeth Yates. These excellent biographies vividly portray the poignant and significant aspects of slavery. Through these books, children can acquire insights into slavery that would be difficult to grasp from even the most accurate and well-written factual books. Fiction should have a central place in lessons on race relations. For example, when the students are studying the concept of "discrimination," a reading of *South Town* and *North Town* by Lorenz Graham will provide meaningful vicarious experiences with this central concept in race relations. Also, no unit on the American black experience would be complete without a study of Negro spirituals. James Weldon Johnson and J. Rosamond Johnson have compiled an excellent collection of them, *The Book of Negro Spirituals*, which is available in a paperback edition. These are just a few suggestions for integrating literature into units or lessons on the black experience.

Several of the items in the second section of the bibliography at the end of this book describe some excellent books written for elementary students. The bibliographies edited by Augusta Baker and Minnie W. Koblitz contain carefully selected lists of fiction, biography, poetry, and folklore, as well as perceptive and helpful evaluative comments. *Interracial Books for Children*, a publication of the Council on Interracial Books for Children, lists and reviews more recent books.

If pupils are in the primary grades or if they have reading disabilities, the teacher may find it necessary to rewrite materials on a level that the students are able to understand. However, there are now a number of black history books, covering all of the historical periods, that most elementary and junior high school students are able to read successfully. The following six books fit into this category:

James A. Banks, *March Toward Freedom: A History of Black Americans*

Arna Bontemps, *One Hundred Years of Negro Freedom*

Joanna Johnson, *Together in America: The Story of Two Races and One Nation*

Earl Schenck Miers, *The Story of the American Negro*

John J. Patrick, *The Progress of the Afro-American*

Carter G. Woodson and Charles H. Wesley, *Negro Makers of History*

In the last two or three years, so many books on the black American designed for elementary and junior high school students have been published that the problem is no longer finding a book, but selecting *quality* books from the large number of mediocre ones that have flooded the market. When there was suddenly a great demand for black history books, many books of dubious quality were hurriedly prepared. Most of these books are poorly researched, written, and illustrated. Thus, before the teacher selects one or more black history books for his students, he should examine them carefully and develop some criteria for selection. The following *criteria questions* should help the teacher evaluate black history books:

1. Is the book accurate? (To be able to judge accuracy, the teacher should consult one of the standard references in the field, such as John Hope Franklin's classic, *From Slavery to Freedom: A History of Negro Americans*.)

2. Is it well written? Will it hold the pupils' interests?

3. Is it well illustrated, either with carefully selected photographs or drawings? Good photographs are superior to poor drawings.

4. Will it withstand the kind of handling likely to be given it by students?

5. Is the type large enough for young children to read easily?

6. Does the book "talk down" to students? Children will not read a book which they feel insults their intelligence. A good book is both sufficiently challenging and rather easily read.

7. Is the book either too easy or too difficult for the students? Although students must be able to read a book without too much difficulty, one that rarely presents them with new words, phrases, insights, and ideas is of dubious educational value.

8. Does the author deal honestly and straightforwardly with controversial topics, or does he evade them?

9. Does the author depict the black American in a "realistic" fashion, or does he perpetuate old stereotypes?

10. Is the book comprehensive? Does it cover in sufficient detail the major periods of the black experience in America?

11. What are the author's qualifications? Is he familiar with *both* the subject matter and with children's learning patterns?

All educational materials should be carefully evaluated before they are purchased, but evaluation must be given special attention when choosing materials for intergroup education. This area of the curriculum is extremely important. Even though there are a number of black history books for middle grade and junior high school students, there is still a scarcity of resources for the primary grades. Also, there are few *excellent* books for the higher grades.

In addition to checking bibliographical sources listed in this book, the teacher should also consult current bibliographies in such sources as *Horn Book, The Children's Guide to Literature, Textbooks in Print,* and the book review sections of newspapers. Major newspapers, such as the *New York Times,* and magazines, such as *Saturday Review,* have periodic supplements devoted entirely to children's books. The teacher should consult these sources because books on the black experience are rapidly rolling off the presses and the newer ones will not be listed in bibliographical sources.

The teacher should carefully study the bibliographical sources at the end of this book. One of the sources is especially recommended —*The Negro Freedom Movement: Past and Present.* It includes films, records, slides, books, tapes, and other audio-visual aids.

When the teacher has compiled his pupils' reading list, which should include books, folklore, fiction, biography, and poetry, he should make a copy of it for each student in the class. Each child should have a personal copy so that he can explore the books and other sources in the school and the public library. This reading list will be treasured by the pupils and will open up for them a whole new and fascinating world of knowledge.

SELF-ANALYSIS OF RACIAL ATTITUDES

Research by Gottlieb, Grambs, Hogan, and others indicate that teachers often have negative attitudes toward Negroes and other minority groups. In many instances the teacher is not aware of his negative disposition toward Negroes. Therefore, before the teacher initiates units or lessons on the black experience, he should examine and clarify his own racial attitudes. A unit taught by a teacher who has an unfavorable attitude toward Negroes may be more harmful than helpful to the children. Unconsciously, the teacher may convey to the students his lack of respect and appreciation for the American black experience.

It is not suggested that a teacher has to be free of racial prejudices before he can successfully teach the black experience, but he should examine and clarify his biases so that he is sufficiently aware of them. By doing this, the teacher will be less likely to convey negative attitudes and beliefs as factual truths to be mastered and believed by the students. In teaching the black experience, it is essential that the teacher make his biases explicit so that the student can accept them for what they are. Otherwise, the pupils may conclude that the teachers' beliefs are facts that should be mastered.

Ermon O. Hogan found that advanced education students could clarify their racial attitudes and biases by writing detailed answers to these three questions.[13]

1. What are the biases which I have toward any ethnic or racial group?
2. What was the source of my biases (parents, peers, school, church, etc.)?
3. What can I do to overcome my biases?

Dr. Hogan reports that students at first complained that they did not have any racial biases and therefore could not answer the questions. However, with her encouragement and assistance all of the students wrote out answers to the questions and found out many things about themselves that they previously would not allow themselves to perceive.

The teacher can employ Dr. Hogan's strategy in attempting to analyze and clarify his racial attitudes and predispositions. Writing out answers to these questions will be therapeutic as well as informative. In addition to utilizing Dr. Hogan's approach to this problem, the teacher may obtain a racial attitude scale and study his own responses to it.[14] Although these suggestions may seem cumbersome at first, they are likely to prove interesting and rewarding. The teacher will undoubtedly learn much about himself and thus be prepared to teach the black experience more effectively.

[13]The author is grateful to Dr. Hogan for sharing her unpublished pioneering research on teacher attitudes and expectations. Her research is in its first phase and will not be published until completed.

[14]See Oscar K. Buros (ed.), *The Fifth Mental Measurements Yearbook* (Highland Park, N.J.: Gryphon Press, 1959).

INITIATING THE UNIT

Ways to initiate a unit or lesson on the black experience can be as varied as the teacher's ingenuity and imagination and the pupils' experiences and interests. The teacher may begin a study of the black experience by asking the pupils to tell him what questions they have about Negroes. The teacher could list these questions on the board. Inasmuch as the students are likely to have many misconceptions, the teacher could ask the students some questions that would illuminate their impressions of Negroes. For example, the teacher may ask the pupils why whites often do not want blacks to live in their neighborhoods, why Negroes often cannot find jobs, and what are the causes of racial outbreaks. Such questions as these will initiate a stimulating discussion and will help the class identify a central problem for study.

Another effective way to begin a study of the black experience is suggested in the Berkeley, California, resource unit, *The History of the Negro in America*. This unit suggests that the teacher ask the pupils to look for information about black Americans in their basal social studies textbook.[15] Because the students will find very little, the teacher should then proceed to ask them to speculate why there is so little material about blacks in their books. From this information the teacher initiates a discussion of famous black Americans. Because of the current interest in the problem, and the urgent racial crisis in our nation, the teacher and the class will be able to devise fascinating ways to initiate a study of the black American experience. A stimulating initiation is a requisite to an effective learning experience.

[15]*The History of the Negro in America* (Berkeley, Cal.: Berkeley Unified School District, 1967), pp. 1–4.

3

Early West Africa: An Anthropological Approach

A unit on the black American should begin with a consideration of his African heritage. Without it, children would not be able to understand the depth and extent of the devastating forces that eroded the Negro's African heritage during the years of slavery. They would also lack the requisite knowledge to fully perceive the consequences of the demise of the Negro's African heritage if they remain unaware of its complexity and sophistication. In other words, children should be exposed to African history and culture if they are to grasp the full significance of the Negro's role in American life. Although all of Africa could justifiably be included, limiting the investigation to West Africa is defensible because the ancestors of most American Negroes came from this area.

A study of Africa is needed to help students dispel any misconceptions they may have about the great continent. Slave traders who went to Africa beginning in the fifteenth century emphasized the "primitive" aspects of African culture. They exaggerated these aspects to create an image of the African as savage, subhuman, and uncivilized. The traders perpetuated this image of the African largely to justify their treatment of African slaves. By arguing that Africans were subhuman, they mitigated their guilt which resulted from

selling and exploiting the aborigines as well as offered a rational-
ization for their behavior. According to Vlahos:

> Men who exploit other men for their material possessions or their
> muscle tend to emphasize the animal in their victims rather than the
> human element. Such an attitude sits more easily on the conscience.
> The slaver must see himself as an ordinary businessman, even a
> benefactor bringing the advantages of civilization to a poor benighted
> heathen folk; . . . No wonder slaving records of the eighteenth and
> nineteenth centuries read rather like commercial transactions, with
> little notice being taken of Africa's people as people, and none at all
> of those people's accomplishment.[1]

The slave traders' concept of the African still exists in American
life, although it has in recent years been challenged. For years the
African has been portrayed as a savage. In order to help children
dispel their misconceptions of Africa, we must help them understand why these stereotypes were formulated and perpetuated. Not
only were they attempts to justify the exploitation of other human
beings, they were also manifestations of the ethnocentrism of Europeans who perceived their culture as superior in every respect to
that of the Africans. They sent missionaries to "civilize" and "save
the souls" of the African aborigines.

To help students evaluate European attitudes toward Africans,
cultural anthropological concepts are needed. One particularly valuable concept is that of *cultural relativism*, advanced by the eminent
anthropologist Ruth Benedict.[2] The gist of this concept is that man
cannot use standards developed in one culture to *justifiably* evaluate
and judge another culture that has developed other means to solve
the problems of survival. Likewise, he cannot determine what is
"primitive" or "normal" in one culture and the society in which it
is embedded on the basis of the standards of another culture.

A study of African culture provides a unique and challenging
opportunity to teach critical anthropological concepts and generalizations. Concepts mastered while studying Africa before the slave
trade began can be used to understand other cultural areas of the
world, particularly other non-Western cultures. Students can more
easily develop respect and appreciation for other cultures if they
are acquainted with the concepts of *culture* and *cultural relativism*.

Although the study of the Negro is undertaken primarily to help
children develop an understanding and appreciation of the Negro's

[1]Olivia Vlahos, *African Beginnings* (New York: Viking Press, 1967), p. 1.
[2]Ruth Benedict, *Patterns of Culture* (New York: Mentor Books, 1959).

role in American life, every opportunity should be taken to help them master critical social science concepts and skills. These goals are by no means mutually exclusive. If a student is able to view African culture in relation to other cultures, he will be more likely to understand and appreciate its high level of development.

THE CONCEPTS OF CULTURE AND CULTURAL RELATIVISM

Hughes defines culture as "... a learned configuration of images and other symbolic elements widely shared among members of a given society which, for individuals, functions as an orientational framework for behavior, and for the group serves as the communicational matrix which tends to coordinate behavior."[3] Lisitzky states that culture is "... all the customs—the different ways of behaving and believing—that each society teaches its members ..."[4] In simplest terms, culture consists of those man-made artifacts, symbols, and institutions that man uses to adjust to his environment. It is man's solution to the problem of survival. Culture is passed on, but not in its entirety, from one generation to the next. Each generation puts its stamp on the culture it inherits. Culture is the phenomenon that distinguishes man from all other animals. According to LaBarre, "... the possession of culture, unique to and universal in man, is the major criterion of the human."[5] The critical point for children to grasp is that culture is a *man-made* system of artifacts and symbols that highly influences his behavior. Since culture is man-made, students will be able to conclude correctly that cultures vary greatly in different parts of the world, in different societies, and among different peoples. Students should also be helped to understand that a cultural system is an organized pattern or whole. Thus, any drastic external or internal changes are likely to disrupt the patterning of a culture. Aware of this concept, students will be more readily able to understand why the exploitation of the African aborigines by white slave traders adversely affected the West African cultural system.

Since cultures are man-made, the cultural relativist assumes that

[3]Charles C. Hughes, "Lectures in Culture and Personality," (East Lansing: Michigan State University, 1968), unpublished.
[4]Gene Lisitzky, *Four Ways of Being Human* (New York: Viking Press, 1956), p. 14.
[5]Weston LaBarre, *The Human Animal* (Chicago: University of Chicago Press, 1954), p. 42.

all cultures are equally valid, and that what is "normal" in human life can vary from culture to culture. A person is frequently considered "normal" in his society if he can function adequately and if most of his characteristics do not differ significantly from those of other people in his culture who are considered to be normal. When the Hopi Indian danced for rain he was considered normal. Such behavior would be considered highly abnormal in most American urban areas. On the other hand, an Arkansas farmer who prayed for a good cotton harvest would not be judged abnormal by most Americans. Ruth Benedict, who was one of America's most eminent anthropologists, felt that the concept of cultural relativity was needed to help develop tolerance of other peoples and cultures.

> Social thinking at the present time has no more important task before it than that of taking adequate account of cultural relativity. . . . We shall arrive then at a more realistic social faith, accepting as grounds of hope and as new bases for tolerance the coexisting and equally valid patterns of life which mankind has created for itself from the raw materials of existence.[6]

If students are exposed to the concepts of *culture* and *cultural relativity* they will be able to approach the study of West African culture with some degree of sophistication and will be able to appreciate the fact that there are *many* ways of being human and that our way of life is only one way, the early African way still another.

For example, pupils in the early and middle grades are likely to perceive the practices of magic and shamanism in early Africa as "strange" or "exotic" if they are not helped to understand what these practices meant to the Africans. To help them understand the "sense" of these institutions, they should be asked to investigate how other cultures have tried to solve the problems that early Africans attempted to solve with magic and shamanism. During such an investigation, the pupils will discover that other cultures have used similar means to solve similar problems. The Hopi Indians, the Eskimos, and many other groups have tried to control the forces of nature with various forms of magic. Through magic, man has been able to mitigate his fears and anxieties and thus function more effectively because of his perceived power over his environment. The pupils will also discover how the early Africans, the Hopi Indians, the Eskimos, present-day Americans, as well as other peoples developed religious rituals to explain perplexing and mystical phenomena.

According to Lisitzky, "At bottom, cultures are man's own peculiar

---

[6]Benedict, *op. cit.*, pp. 239–40.

way of adapting himself to the special conditions of his environment—in short, of meeting the challenge of survival."[7] Universally, man has faced similar problems of survival, and has often devised similar means to solve them. However, he has frequently used highly diversified means to meet the challenges of survival. *By studying early West African culture, and by comparing it with other cultures, including our own, students will be able to see man's great capacity to adapt and to create diverse cultures.*

> Any acquaintance with anthropology is . . . bound to awaken a feeling of pride in the human race, in the inexhaustible fertility of its power to create cultures. With that comes tolerance. We may not care to adopt the customs of another culture for ourselves, but they are never again so likely to strike us as "wrong" or "ugly" or "immoral." . . . We see that they were come by precisely as we come by ours, that it is only a matter of how one is brought up. What may possibly seem wrong is the act of needlessly imposing by force the customs of one culture on another.[8]

In addition to helping students develop tolerance for other cultures, a study of early West Africa should help them better understand themselves, by becoming acquainted with the notion that they are a product of their culture. The very fact that children may, if not properly guided, at first perceive a shaman's behavior as strange indicates the extent of their own cultural biases.

UNIVERSALS IN HUMAN CULTURES

Although many of the problems of survival have been solved in different ways in different cultures, many human institutions and modes of adaptation are highly similar. Thus, a study of the African background would not only enable students to discover the ways in which early Africans were culturally different from other peoples, but it would also help them become acquainted with the ways in which their adaptations were similar to other human societies, including our own.

Social scientists have found that certain institutions exist in all human cultures, although these institutions often take diverse forms. Such institutions are called *cultural universals*. One of the universal human institutions is the family. Every society has some form of family life. In trying to account for the universality of human institutions, social scientists have hypothesized that such institutions are human responses to the universal biological needs of man. LaBarre,

[7]Lisitzky, *op. cit.*, p. 17.
[8]*Ibid.*, p. 20.

in his book *The Human Animal,* suggests that the emergence of the human family was largely a response to man's perennial sex drive and to the physical dependence of the human infant. He writes:

> The anthropoid and the human male alike stays to form a family not because of extraneous cultural or moral fiats after the fact, but because biologically speaking he *wants to;* not because of any tender and special *ad hoc* paternal instinct toward the helpless little ones but because of powerful organic drives within him toward the female.[9]

Social scientists have likewise explained other human universals in terms of response to man's biological needs and drives. For example, the *incest taboo* exists in all human societies. Social scientists hypothesize that this taboo is universal because sexual relations between parents and progeny would be disruptive to the family. Extramarital relations are also universally prohibited, except under special prescribed circumstances. Social scientists also explain this prohibition as protective of the family. These explanations are *hypotheses.* Although they appear to be reasonable, they have not been verified.

Berelson and Steiner summarize the most significant behavioral science research. Among the human universals they list are these:

(a) Despite the extreme range in human cultures, certain similarities in socialization do exist across them.

(b) There is a tendency for parents to raise their children the way they were raised, although they may be unaware that they are doing so.

(c) Severity of socialization seems to make for generalized anxiety in later life.[10]

In their study of Africa, students should be led to discover the different ways by which man can become human. They should also be helped to perceive the universal problems that man faces and the frequently similar ways that men of different cultures have devised to solve these problems. Students should be helped to discover that all human societies have a compelling desire to explain the complex phenomena of the universe and to exert some measure of control over nature. If students are aware of this generalization, they will be able to appreciate and understand the functions of the shamans among the Eskimo, the witchdoctors among the Africans, the medicine men

[9]LaBarre, *op. cit.,* p. 104.
[10]Bernard Berelson and Gary A. Steiner, *Human Behavior: An Inventory of Scientific Findings* (New York: Harcourt, Brace & World, 1964), pp. 71–76.

among the American Indians, and such things as water witching in our own society.

THE INQUIRY APPROACH TO THE STUDY OF AFRICA

Students should use an inquiry approach in their study of West Africa. In the problem-solving model presented in Chapter 1, it was pointed out that students must first identify a problem and state it in clear, precise terms before they can begin to inquire. Such problems are usually stated as questions. The teacher should assume the major responsibility for helping the class to state problems in precise terms because the quality of the questions limits the kinds of discoveries that can be made.

The students should also be aware of the value judgments and assumptions that influence the methods they utilize, their criteria for evaluating sources, and the conclusions they derive. Goldmark has developed an inquiry model that emphasizes the importance of *inquiry into inquiry,* that is, of inquiring into the methods used in the original inquiry. Her model is reproduced below because it illuminates the importance of considering the *assumptions* we make when inquiring and the values that go into our judgments. Utilizing this model, students will continually assess the methods used to reach conclusions, consider alternative methods, and evaluate the criteria used in accepting or rejecting evidence.

I. Understanding the Problem.
   A. Recognizing that there is a problem.
   B. Abducting alternative hypotheses.
   C. Gathering data.
   D. Organizing data.
   E. Organizing and analyzing each alternative.
II. Identifying Criteria for Judgment of Each Alternative.
III. Identifying Values and Assumptions of the Alternatives.
IV. Inquiry into Inquiry.
   A. Reorganizing data into discourses and categories; identifying the language and methods used.
   B. Revisiting assumptions and expanding inquiry with new hypotheses.
   C. Inquiring into the method used, the criteria and values of the method, and possible alternative methods.[11]

[11]From *Social Studies: A Method of Inquiry* by Bernice Goldmark, pp. 129–30. © 1968 by Wadsworth Publishing Company, Inc., Belmont, California 94002. Reprinted by permission of the publisher. The model is presented here in slightly abbreviated form.

In regard to her model, Goldmark writes, "Awareness of, and inquiry into, methods is essential if the methods are to be applied again or if they are to be reconstructed. It is only when we question what we did, how we did it, why we did it this way, and if we *should* do it this way, that inquiry is continually expanded."[12]

Before students can inquire about any area of knowledge or be able to formulate meaningful questions and hypotheses in that area, they must have some familiarity with the subject matter. The students can acquire the requisite knowledge for beginning to inquire about early Africa by reading books, viewing films and filmstrips, examining artifacts, and taking notes on information supplied by the teacher. While they are gaining the required familiarity with the subject, they should master the concepts of culture, cultural relativity, and the notion that there are many ways of being human. If students have mastered these concepts, they will be able to formulate more useful questions.

SOURCES FOR INVESTIGATION

After the students have formulated appropriate questions and hypotheses, they should begin to study and evaluate the sources they will use in finding answers to their queries and in confirming or rejecting their hypotheses.

In trying to answer questions and confirm or reject hypotheses, students should be encouraged to use many different sources, such as letters, newspapers, travel accounts, art objects, textbooks, and films. The variety of sources that can be used in a study of early West Africa is obviously limited. Textbooks, especially those for the middle grades, include very little information about West Africa or exclude it altogether. Texts that do have material on West Africa often give a distorted picture of it. Such books should not be withheld from students, for they can be used to teach them to make critical evaluations of the materials they use and to encourage them to make judgments about the accuracy and reliability of sources. Since pupils will encounter conflicting interpretations, they should always be encouraged to examine the writer's background, basic assumptions, and his reasons for writing. They should also consider the audience he had in mind. By seeking this kind of information, students will be more readily able to evaluate particular facts and interpretations. Students

[12]*Ibid.*, p. 119.

should always be encouraged to reach their own conclusions through reflection and investigation. No matter how strong a student's biases are, he should be encouraged to make his conclusions on the basis of the evidence at hand. He should also be encouraged to responsibly defend his judgments and to accept their consequences.

Although the kinds of materials on early West Africa are limited, they are not more limited than materials for some other historical periods. The teacher must play a vital role in gathering materials for student investigation. The teacher's role will vary with the maturity and experiences of the children. For children in the lower grades, the teacher may have to supply most of the reading materials. He can read adult and children's books on Africa and then rewrite those portions of them he wishes to use in a form that can be understood by his pupils. Few books have been written on Africa for the very young child. For students in the middle and upper grades the teacher can purchase books for the room library and he can also give his students a reading list. Recommended children's books on West Africa are described in the annotated bibliographies listed at the end of this book. He can also direct the students to the local museum in their study of Africa. Most major museums have displays related to life in early West Africa as well as West African art and sculpture.

The first Europeans who went to West Africa were traders who were not especially interested in West African culture. Even so, the earliest primary sources on early Africa are the accounts written by these traders. If they are used in class, these sources should not be censored. However, they are likely to give an unbalanced view of West Africa if the students are not cautioned to read them critically and if they are not used along with other sources that present early Africa from another point of view. No matter how critically students read, they are greatly handicapped in trying to find answers to their queries if *all* their sources are biased in the same direction. When students are reading these sources, they should know that the slave traders were frequently seeking justifications for their exploitation of other human beings.

Among more recent documents are the accounts written by Leo Frobenius, an ethnologist who made African expeditions from 1910 to 1912. He brought to his study of Africa no preconceived notions of the inferiority of native cultures. [13] Also, historians are amassing mate-

---

[13]Leslie H. Fishel, Jr., and Benjamin Quarles, *The Negro American: A Documentary History* (Glenview, Ill.: Scott, Foresman, 1967), p. 8.

rials written before the Portuguese went to Africa in the fifteenth century. These materials will become increasingly available. The teacher will find other sources listed in the bibliography.

A READING PROGRAM FOR THE TEACHER

The teacher should plan a reading program for himself in both West African history and cultural anthropology if he is to effectively utilize the approach suggested in this chapter. He should also examine children's books in order to become familiar with these materials. *Four Ways of Being Human* by Gene Lisitzky will give both the teacher and the pupils an excellent introduction to cultural anthropology and the concept of *culture*. This book was written for students in the upper elementary grades because the author felt a need for elementary school children like her daughter to have an introduction to cultural anthropology. So far, professional anthropologists have shown little interest in writing books for children. Until they do, teachers will have to follow Lisitzky's example—that is, do their own reading in anthropology and write what they have learned on a level that can be understood by children.

The teacher should not confine his readings to materials written primarily for children because the concepts in children's books are often superficial or distorted. The teacher will not always be aware of this fact unless he has read more reliable sources.

Ruth Benedict's *Patterns of Culture* is lucid and well written, and it contains what is probably the best statement of the concept of *cultural relativity* that is available. This book, like the other books recommended below, is available in an inexpensive paperback edition. *Mirror for Man* by Clyde Kluckhohn should also be a part of the teacher's reading program. Two other anthropology books especially recommended for teachers are *The Study of Anthropology* by Pertti J. Pelto and *Invitation to Anthropology* by Douglas L. Oliver. These books will give the teacher some insight into the nature of anthropology as a discipline. A book that describes social science research techniques that the teacher will find helpful in guiding pupil inquiries is *The Tools of Social Science* by John Madge. It contains information on the documentation of evidence and on methodologies used in social science research.

In addition to reading in cultural anthropology, the teacher should examine several comprehensive West African histories. Especially recommended is *An Introduction to the History of West Africa* by

J. D. Page. Two other good histories are available in paperback: *Africa and Africans* by Paul Bohannan is a comprehensive history of Africa from its beginnings to the present; *A History of West Africa* by Basil Davidson traces the history of West Africa up to nineteenth-century European colonialism. The teacher will also find chapters on West Africa in comprehensive black history books. John Hope Franklin devotes three chapters to the subject in *From Slavery to Freedom.*

ORGANIZING CONTENT

If the learning experiences are to be meaningful, the teacher must assume the main responsibility for formulating clear objectives in behavioral terms so that their attainment or nonattainment can be easily ascertained. With the help of the class, the teacher should set up objectives in both the cognitive and affective domains. The objectives chosen will directly influence the selection of the content of the unit.

Some cognitive objectives considered important by this writer have already been pointed out in the preceding sections of this chapter. These objectives are partially summarized in these statements: (1) The students should be able to state clearly the various ways by which man has become human in various societies; (2) the students should be able to state examples illustrating the fact that there are infinite ways of being human; (3) the students should be able to demonstrate, orally or in writing, how early West Africa is an example of a cultural area;[14] (4) the students should be able to state the advantages of viewing a human culture from a "cultural relativistic" perspective; (5) the students should be able to state why the early slave traders emphasized the less developed (as perceived by the Europeans) aspects of West African culture. These objectives by no means exhaust the possible ones that can be formulated while considering early West Africa from an anthropological perspective; they are merely samples of important objectives that can be stated in behavioral terms.

So far we have made little mention of the selection of content for

[14]Although I refer to early West Africa as one culture, it was actually made up of many different cultures. The common elements of these cultures can be emphasized, but students should know that the cultural regions often differed widely in some aspects. For example, Africa has more than eight-hundred native languages.

the study of West Africa, which should not be selected and outlined until the objectives have been specified. The students should have the opportunity to learn about the highly developed states of early West Africa. They should also find out about the kings who ruled these empires. When the Arabs traveled to West Africa in the seventh century they found civilizations that had existed for centuries. The early African states of Ghana, Mali, and Songhai should be discussed at some length. Askia the Great, Mansa Musa, and Sunni Ali are among the West African kings who should be considered. Thus, one of the major objectives for the study of early West Africa can be stated: The students should be able to list the great states of early West Africa, their kings, and their general characteristics.

In addition to studying the highly developed states, the students should also be introduced to life in the less developed states. They should learn how some communities were organized around families or clans. Students should consider the economic system, the religious system, the organization of the family, magic, rites and ceremonies, art, literature, and music. If students are to grasp the concept that there are many ways of being human and that early African culture was one way, they must also be exposed to other cultures. Thus, the teacher should encourage the students to compare and contrast Africa's culture and institutions with the institutions of other pre-literate cultures as well as with our own. Both differences and similarities should be pointed out. When the students read that early Africans sometimes sacrificed slaves or animals to appease their gods or ancestors, they should also be led to discover that the Aztecs of Central Mexico also sacrificed men to appease their gods. The students should be encouraged to speculate about possible reasons for both the similarities and differences in various cultures.

A study of Africa should include some information about where and how man first developed. Recent evidence by Louis B. Leakey and other anthropologists indicates that man's birthplace was Africa. There are several reasons why man's origins should be considered during a study of early Africa: (1) This is an excellent opportunity to introduce children to the idea that man evolved and did not spring full blown from the earth, as some children believe; (2) this is also an excellent opportunity to introduce children to the concept of *theory* and how social scientists modify theories when new evidence is discovered; (3) children are likely to develop more humanistic attitudes toward all peoples if they realize that mankind had a common beginning and that all men are biologically related.

OBJECTIVES IN THE AFFECTIVE DOMAIN

In addition to formulating objectives in the cognitive domain, the teacher should specify objectives in the affective domain. If properly guided, students will develop an appreciation for early West African culture and institutions. They will also develop positive attitudes toward Africa in general. The pupils should be exposed to African folklore, music, and art. They should also investigate Western art, literature, and music to find ways in which African culture has influenced Western artists and writers. Children are bound to be fascinated with African folklore and art. The teacher may find it valuable to plan a field trip to a local museum and to ask the museum director to plan a lecture for the children on African art forms.

In the classroom, the teacher can reinforce the lecture given by the art director by showing slides, pictures, and, if possible, actual African art objects. If the teacher or the pupils know anyone in the community who has traveled in Africa, the class could invite this person to talk to the class about present-day Africa and to bring any African souvenirs he may have. The class should make use of the talents of people in the community. Many citizens will have slides, books, or other articles that they would be happy to share with the class. The students should be made aware of the fact that the visitor is describing modern Africa rather than early Africa; however, they will discover that Africa's culture today still reflects the legacy of the past in many ways. They should be asked to make some conclusions about historical elements that are still exerting an influence on Africa today.

EVALUATION

If the objectives of the unit have been stated in clear behavioral terms, evaluation will be greatly facilitated, although the teacher will still have to determine some minimum level of acceptable performance. This level of acceptable performance should be communicated to the pupils before they are asked to perform. Evaluation should continue throughout the study of Africa and should include not only written examinations but oral reports, role-playing exercises, the building of replicas, and other projects.

In order to ascertain achievement in the affective domain, the teacher can construct and administer a racial attitude scale, similar to the one presented in Chapter 2. Pupils are likely to experience a marked change in attitudes toward Africa if they have brought negative attitudes and misconceptions about it to the classroom. The teacher should also note the pupils' informal comments before and after the study of Africa. Determining whether students can correctly identify African art forms is another way of assessing attitude change. If the students have cared enough to learn to correctly identify African art forms from a collection of African and non-African art forms, they most likely appreciate the African art forms.

Because of the racial conflict in our nation, it is urgent that we help children develop respect and appreciation for the black American and his culture. We must begin by helping them to understand and appreciate the Negro's African heritage. Studying early West Africa will not only help children to appreciate other world cultures, but will help them gain a deserved respect for the black man's rich and diverse past. Helping children attain these goals will help minimize the increasing racial polarization in our nation.

4

Slavery: Historical Inquiry

One important objective of the social studies program should be to help students understand the methods used by writers of history. Another objective is to make them aware that written history is a record of events presented from the point of view of the person who wrote it. This approach will help students realize that different writers will treat a given event in different ways. By helping students to understand how history is written, we can help them learn to appreciate the difficulty involved in reconstructing past events accurately.

Some excellent materials to use in helping students understand the importance of the historian's point of view are the accounts of slavery in the United States. The versions written by Northern and Southern historians often conflict. A slave's account of slavery can be expected to differ from an account by a slaveowner. Not even all slaves viewed slavery in the same way, as the two following accounts by former slaves reveal.

Account I

Then he chains all he slaves round the necks and fastens the chains to the hosses and makes them walk all the way to Texas. My mother and my sister had to walk. Emma was my sister. Somewhere on the road it went to snowing, and Massa wouldn't let us wrap anything round our feet. We had to sleep on the ground, too, in all that snow.

Massa have a great, long whip platted out of rawhide, and when one the niggers fall behind or give out, he hit him with that whip. It takes the hide every time he hit a nigger. Mother, she give out on the way, 'bout the line of Texas. Her feet got raw and bleeding, and her legs swoll plumb out of shape. Then Massa, he just take out he gun and shot her, and whilst she lay dying he kicks her two-three times and say, "Damn nigger what can't stand nothing." Boss, you know that man, he wouldn't bury mother, just leave her laying where he shot her at. You know, then there wasn't no law 'gainst killing nigger slaves.[1]

Account II

I stayed with my ma every night, but my mistress raised me. My ma had to work hard, so every time Old Mistress thought we little black children was hungry 'tween meals she would call us up to the house to eat. Sometime she would give us johnnycake and plenty of butter-milk to drink with it. They had a long trough for us that they would keep so clean. They would fill this trough with buttermilk, and all us children would git round the trough and drink with our mouths and hold our johnnycake with our hands. I can just see myself drinking now. It was so good. There was so many black folks to cook for that cooking was done outdoors. Greens was cooked in a big black washpot just like you boils clothes in now . . . But we didn't eat out of plates. We et out of gourds and had homemade wood spoons. And we had plenty to eat. Whooo-ee! Just plenty to eat. Old Master's folks raised plenty of meat, and they raise their sugar, rice, peas, chickens, eggs, cows and just everything good to eat.[2]

When using documents of this nature, the teacher could ask the class questions like these:

1. What kind of person do you think wrote Account I? Account II?
2. How are the two accounts alike? How are they different?
3. Assume that you are a historian who is writing on how masters treated their slaves. The two accounts are your only source material. What problems would you encounter? What conclusions would you reach?

Another way to make students aware that history is written from special points of view and that these points of view change with the times is to ask them to examine the way that the subject of slavery is handled in textbooks written at different periods of time or in different parts of the country. The purpose of such exercises is to help students understand that history is written by people who are influenced by many different things. Exercises of this kind will help

---

[1] "Ben Simpson: Georgia and Texas," in B. A. Botkin, ed., *Lay My Burden Down: A Folk History of Slavery* (Chicago: University of Chicago Press, 1945, 1965), p. 75. Copyright © 1945, 1965 by University of Chicago Press.
[2] "Millie Evans: North Carolina," in Botkin, *op. cit.*, p. 61.

students to understand that historians from different regions write about events in different ways and that it is natural that they should do so.

EXAMPLE OF AN INQUIRY LESSON ON SLAVERY

A class of seventh grade black pupils analyzed a series of historical materials that their teacher had provided. The documents were slightly edited and simplified so that they could be read more easily. Some of the material that these seventh graders used is reproduced below.

> . . . the negro race is inferior to the white race, and living in their midst, they would be far outstripped or outwitted in the chase of free competition. Gradual but certain extermination would be their fate.[3]

> . . . [Negroes] were born slaves of barbarian masters, untaught in all of the useful arts and occupations, reared in heathen darkness, and sold by heathen masters . . . They were transferred to shores enlightened by rays of Christianity.[4]

> . . . On last Monday week, I had to whip Polly for her impudence to me . . . I regret it very much but there must be one master in a family or there can be no peace. I told her that she should never be sold . . . provided she would behave herself . . . she still tells me that she is perfectly willing to be sold.[5]

> Mr. Severe was rightly named; he was a cruel man. I have seen him whip a woman, causing the blood to run half an hour at the time; and this, too, in the midst of her crying children, pleading for their mother's release . . .[6]

In addition to reading primary sources, the pupils examined excerpts from history books, such as the following:

> The white Southerners who supported the system of slavery were not necessarily wicked men. They inherited the system from their fathers. For two reasons they were afraid to end it: First, the raising of cotton and other crops on which the South depended required cheap labor. Second, white people feared the poor and uneducated Negro millions.

[3]George Fitzhugh, "Negro Slavery," in Merle Curti, Willard Thorp, and Carlos Baker (eds.), *American Issues: The Social Record* (New York: J. B. Lippincott, 1960), p. 522.

[4]Jefferson Davis, *The Rise and Fall of the Confederate Government* (New York: Crowell-Collier, 1961), p. 329.

[5]See Vincent R. Rogers, "Using Source Materials with Children," *Social Education*, 24 (1960), pp. 307–09.

[6]Frederick Douglass, "The Plight of the Slaves," *The Negro in American Life: Selected Readings* (Boston: Houghton Mifflin, 1965), p. 27.

White men did not know how to deal with Negroes except as their masters.[7]

. . . American slavery [was] the most awful the world has ever known . . . The slave was totally removed from the protection of organized society (compare the elaborate provisions for the protection of slaves in the Bible) and his existence as a human being was given no recognition by any religious or secular agency.[8]

. . . In the sale of slaves there was the persistent practice of dividing families. Husbands were separated from wives, and mothers were separated from their children. There was never any respect shown for the slave family.[9]

The pupils also read *I, Juan de Pareja* by Elizabeth B. De Trevino, *Up From Slavery* by Booker T. Washington, *The Book of American Negro Spirituals* by James Weldon Johnson and J. Rosamond Johnson, as well as *Amos Fortune: Free Man* by Elizabeth Yates, a poignant book that vividly depicts the horrors of slavery and the dehumanization of the slaves by the early American slave traders.

They read a poem by Phillis Wheatley who wrote about her own experience as a slave in the United States. It begins:

> No more America in mournful strain
> Of wrongs, and grievance unredress'd complain,
> No longer shall thou dread the iron chain,
> Which wanton Tyranny with lawless hand
> Has made, and which it meant t' enslave the land.[10]

The pupils read the primary sources, the sections from history books, and the biographical and fictional works to help them solve the problem that they had identified, "What was black slavery like in the United States?" Their teacher had helped them define their problem in clear, specific terms. With the teacher's guidance, the class then formulated specific questions related to their central problem. These are some of the questions:

How were the slaves treated?

How did people who were not slaves feel about slavery?

[7]Ralph C. Preston and John Tottle, *In These United States* (Lexington, Mass.: Raytheon Education Company, 1969), p. 171.

[8]Nathan Glazer, "Introduction," in Stanley M. Elkins, *Slavery: A Problem in American Institutional and Intellectual Life* (New York: Grosset & Dunlap, 1963), p. ix.

[9]John Hope Franklin, *From Slavery to Freedom: A History of Negro Americans* (New York: Knopf, 1967), pp. 178–79.

[10]From "Phillis Wheatley's Poem on Her Own Slavery," *Eyewitness: The Negro in American History.* William L. Katz, ed., (New York: Pitman, 1967), p. 39.

How did slavery in the United States compare with slavery in other parts of the world?

How hard did the slaves have to work?

How did master and slave feel toward each other?

Did slaves ever escape?

After the pupils had identified their problem and formulated specific questions related to it, the teacher asked them to tell what they thought black slavery had been like in the United States. They had picked up ideas about slavery from textbooks used in previous grades, from biographical and fictional works they had read, from the mass media, and from discussions they had heard about slavery from their parents and grandparents. The pupils had many erroneous notions about slavery, such as:

Many slaves were happy and contented.

A few slaves were treated badly, but most were well treated.

Most slaves worked on large plantations rather than on small farms.

Everyone except slaveowners was against slavery.

Slavery in the United States was just like slavery in other parts of the world.

After telling the teacher their notions of black slavery, the pupils read the documents their teacher had prepared for them and they searched for other sources in the school and room libraries. They viewed films and filmstrips on black slavery, told about accounts of slavery that had been handed down in their families, and role-played a slave auction and the Vesey slave rebellion.

In reading the documents the class encountered conflicting accounts of slavery. In one source they read that slaves were "transferred to shores enlightened by rays of Christianity"; in another they read that compared with other slavery systems, "American slavery was the most awful the world has ever known." It is difficult to accept both of these statements as historical facts. The pupils felt that if black slavery in North America was "the most awful the world has ever known," slaves were not in a land "enlightened by rays of Christianity." Ascertaining the validity and reliability of the sources proved most challenging for the pupils. With the teacher's guidance, the class made up a list of questions that they used as a guide in ascertaining the value of the various sources in helping them to discover what black slavery was *really* like in America. They asked such questions as:

In what region of the country did the author live?
For what purpose was the author writing?
What audience did the author have in mind?
What were the author's probable biases?
What were the author's training and qualifications?
When was the document written?
Does the author often use emotionally laden words?
How does his account compare with others that we have read?
Does the author cite sufficient evidence to support his conclusions?
Does the author base his arguments on fact or opinion?
What was the author's social class?
What was the author's race?
What are the author's basic assumptions about slavery?
What are the author's basic assumptions about black people?
Are the assumptions sufficiently supported by data?

After answering these kinds of questions about the sources they had read, the pupils were able to generalize about the nature of history and the extent to which history has been written to support racist views. They concluded that because the historian can never discover all of the information about any single event or present all of the data that he uncovers, he must use some criterion for selection. They discovered that his selection is influenced by his personal bias, his reasons for writing, and by the society and times in which he lives and works. The discrepancies found in the accounts of black slavery that the pupils read were classical illustrations of the impact of cultural, racial, and regional influences on written history.

The teacher of this seventh grade class used the topic of slavery to help his pupils develop inquiry and problem-solving skills. Such skills enable students to understand the difficulties inherent in establishing historical "accuracy," and help them to read history more critically.

In order to prepare our students for an increasingly interdependent world, we must expose them to a broad view of history. We should teach students to examine historical writings critically and expose the students to the methods of the historian. With this approach to the teaching of black history, we can develop critically minded citizens for a world in which the ability to think and to solve problems will be essential for the survival of our nation's democratic ideals.

5

Civil War and Reconstruction: Inquiry and Simulation

The Civil War, or the War Between the States, was one of the bloodiest wars in the history of this country. The causes of the Civil War have probably been discussed as much as any event in our history. Determining *causes* in history is very difficult because the historian cannot go back in time to observe past events. He must rely on artifacts, letters, diaries, and other written accounts in his attempts to reconstruct the past.

The records that the historian must use are never complete and they often have large gaps. They were written by people who saw things in their own way. As we pointed out in Chapter 4, the accounts of slavery written by Northerners who visited the South during the nineteenth century were very different from accounts written by people who lived in the South. When a historian reads records that conflict, he chooses those accounts that he regards as most nearly accurate or he weighs one account against the other. What the historian selects to write as history is greatly influenced by his cultural background, audience, and the times in which he lives.

Northern and Southern historians have written very different accounts of the Civil War; these accounts reflect the regions in which each group of historians lived. More than a hundred years have passed since the Civil War ended, but books about it are still flowing off the presses. The wounds from the long struggle from 1861 to 1865 are still evident in the way that Northerners and Southerners often feel and act toward each other. Many of our racial problems today have their roots in the aftermath of the Civil War.

There is no complete agreement about the causes of the Civil

War, but many historians believe that slavery was the single most important issue. They also believe that the war had many other causes. For instance, Charles Beard's opinion that the struggle was largely a result of conflicts in economic interests is still accepted by some historians. Perhaps the safest statement to make, in light of current historical research, is that although the Civil War had many causes, slavery was the most important cause. However, this interpretation might change when new evidence is uncovered. Because of the changing nature of historical interpretations, students will benefit from examining some of these changing interpretations while they are studying the Civil War period. However, before they examine any documents that present conflicting interpretations regarding the causes of the Civil War, students should become familiar with the nature of historical research. After studying the nature of history, the students will realize that different accounts can be written about *any* event, and that most historical accounts are made up of statements written by people who have different points of view. The activities presented in the following section will help students become familiar with the nature of historical research.

ACTIVITIES

1. Compare the methods used by historians to solve historical problems with the methods used by natural scientists, such as chemists and biologists, to solve problems in natural science. How do the methods differ? How are they similar? Is history a social *science*? Why or why not? Do value judgments go into the selection of problems that historians study? Do they go into the selection of problems that natural scientists study? Is the *scientific method* itself based on certain value judgments and assumptions about the world and the nature of man?

2. The basic steps of the scientific method are listed below. What problems does the historian face when he applies this method to historical inquiry?

   a. identifying the problem
   b. defining the problem in clear, specific terms
   c. developing hypotheses
   d. gathering data
   e. analyzing data
   f. drawing conclusions relative to the hypotheses
   g. identifying values and assumptions of the method used

3. At least two students are needed for this problem. Each one should write an account of an event or a program that he has observed or attended. The accounts should be written independently. When the reports have been written, ask the class to compare them to see how they are alike and how they differ. The class should use these two reports to answer the following questions:

a. Can different accounts be written about the same event?
b. What does the answer to question (a) tell us about the writing of history?
c. Are two people who witness an automobile accident likely to give identical reports of it?
d. Are two historians who read the same documents about a particular historical event likely to write identical accounts of the event? Why or why not?
e. Are two people who participate in or observe the same historical event likely to write identical accounts of the event? Why or why not?
f. What are some of the factors that cause historians to write differing accounts of the same historical events?

4. Help your students locate several accounts of the Civil War written by Northern and Southern historians. Ask them the following questions: How are the accounts alike? How do they differ? Are there any contradictions in the accounts? If so, why?

5. After your students complete one or more of the exercises above, ask them to write several *generalizations* about the nature and writing of history. They should state the *limitations* of the generalizations which they derive.

SIMULATION: THE RECONSTRUCTION GAME

A simulation activity is a dynamic exercise that utilizes a model of a real-life situation. Students are asked to make decisions for a given time period. The results of the decisions are discussed, and then decisions are made for the next time period. For example, for a one-hour game period students may make decisions concerning events that took place in the South between 1861 and 1865. During a second hour of the game the players could make decisions on events that took place between 1866 and 1877. Thus time is compressed and events that occurred over a period of years may be simulated in a few hours.

Simulation gives students an opportunity to learn from experience without paying the price that might result from unwise decisions made in real life. Simulation games are played according to game rules because people must live their lives within the restrictive framework of society's norms and laws. In the exercise, the outcome of a person's life may be anticipated. Simulation exercises are used in a variety of fields for just such anticipatory purposes.

Effective teacher guidance is necessary for maximum benefits to accrue from simulation activities. Games may encourage conformist attitudes if they are not properly planned and executed. Also, some students may be able to figure out too much about the game. Moreover, too great an emphasis on winning may destroy the purpose of the game. To minimize these possibilities, the teacher must use simulation as an integral part of the regular course of study. Used in isolation, simulation activities are of little value. The games should be used only with a clear understanding by both teachers and pupils of the contribution that they can make to the major unit object-ives.

Simulation exercises can be incorporated into units on race relations and black history in a variety of ways. They can be used at the beginning of units both as icebreakers and as orientation activities. Games can be played more than once, both before and after a problem or concept has been introduced. The following steps will facilitate the introduction of a game:

1. Define simulation for the students.
2. Give the students a brief history of simulation.
3. Point out the limitations of simulation games, or ask the students to state ways in which games may be limiting.
4. Explain the purpose of the game.
5. Conduct an item-by-item review of the forms included in the game.
6. Have a question-and-answer period regarding the game. All questions, of course, should not be answered. Answering all questions will reduce the game's challenging potential. If students complain because certain questions are not answered, an explanation stating that their questions are a part of the game's problem will usually prove satisfactory.

The following sources will further acquaint the teacher with simulation theory and describe other games:

Sarane S. Boocock and E. D. Schild (eds.), *Simulation Games in Learning* (Beverly Hills: Sage Publications, 1968)

Elliot Carlson, *Learning Through Games* (Washington, D.C.: Public Affairs Press, 1968)

June R. Chapin, "Simulation Games," *Social Education,* 32 (December, 1968), pp. 798–99, 803 ff.

Arthur J. Hogan, "Simulation: An Annotated Bibliography," *Social Education,* 32 (March, 1968), pp. 242–44

Daniel Roselle (ed.), "Simulation: The Game Explosion," *Social Education,* 33 (February, 1969), pp. 176–99. Articles in this special issue on simulation include "Simulation in the Social Studies: An Overview," by Samuel Brodbelt; "Simulation Games in the Social Studies: The 'Reality' Issue," by Howard Kardatzke; "Simulations and Changes in Racial Attitudes," by Paul DeKock; "Organizing Simulated Environments," by Philip M. Burgess, Lawrence E. Peterson, and Carl D. Frantz; "Simulation: The Game of 'Section'," by Angus M. Gunn; and "The Foreign Policy Association Bibliography on Simulation."

The game discussed in this chapter deals with the Reconstruction Period. It was created to help a class of seventh grade students become more aware of some of the problems that faced the South immediately after the Civil War. When students read about Reconstruction, it often has little meaning for them because it took place more than a hundred years ago and was experienced by people who are very remote from their lives. The Reconstruction Game placed the students in an environment where they faced problems similar to those of the South after the Civil War and gave them an opportunity to actively participate in a simulated reconstruction of the South. The Reconstruction Period became real for this class.

Throughout the game students were asked to make decisions that affected their political, educational, and economic status. Their decisions not only influenced their own lives, but the lives of others in their simulated society. Thus the students were given opportunities to understand how and why certain decisions were made during Reconstruction and why others were not made, and to formulate alternative plans that were more effective than the plan devised by the Reconstruction government in 1867. Through their own decision-making strategies students were able to devise alternative plans, execute them, and to witness their outcomes.

Before the game was played, the students read about the Reconstruction Period. They were not only introduced to the legislative program that was used to reconstruct the South, but they were also given information on alternative reconstruction programs that were proposed by both Northerners and Southerners who sympathized with the fate of the former Confederacy. These readings helped the students to attain the knowledge that was necessary for them to play the game effectively. In addition, it provided them with valuable insights regarding alternative reconstruction plans. Knowledge of alternative plans served as a departure point for student creativity.

Each of the 30 students in the class was assigned a role in the game. The roles included legislators, freedmen, Southern aristocrats, poor whites, carpetbaggers, and scalawags. The three students who were not assigned historical roles served as game coordinators. The freedmen, aristocrats, poor whites, scalawags, and carpetbaggers were all active players. Their goal was to accumulate points within the framework of the legislators' reconstruction plan. Each player tried to accumulate as many points as possible, creating an element of competition. The students who played freedmen, aristocrats, poor whites, scalawags, and carpetbaggers were given profiles of people who could have lived during the Reconstruction Period. They were asked to assume the role of that person and to make decisions for him.

In order to create a setting wherein students would experience conflicts similar to those experienced by Southerners during the Reconstruction period, they were given differing amounts of education, and political and economic power. This power was actualized by assigning each player a specific number of points. The players understood that their goal was to try to increase their number of points. However, this had to be done within the legal framework set up by the legislature. Players could increase their points by increasing their amounts of education, political power, or economic power. In general, persons with higher social status had more points at the beginning of the game. For example, poor whites had more points than freedmen, and the aristocracy had more points than poor whites. Upper-status persons faced fewer barriers than lower-status individuals. Freedmen and poor whites could not attend public schools until the legislature passed a special bill permitting them to do so.

The legislators simulated the members of the United States Congress. Their goal was to develop a program of reconstruction for the South. As their program was developed, it was passed on to the players, via the blackboard, as the law of the land. They did not, however, have the option of modifying the program after receiving feedback from the players. The legislators created their own strategies for reconstruction. However, they became thoroughly acquainted with the situation in Congress and in the South following the Civil War and prior to Reconstruction. They were encouraged to explore different ideas and to discover new concepts and strategies.

Although the legislators played an active and significant role in the game, they did not compete with the other players for points. This freed them from obvious conflicts of interest and gave them an opportunity to make sound and effective legislative decisions.

The legislators were divided into two groups, which were called Republicans and Democrats. Each group had varying degrees of power. Legislative power was actualized by allowing each legislator to control varying numbers of votes in the legislature. Each legislator drew a number at the beginning of the game and this number determined how many votes he had in the legislature. The maximum number was five and the minimum was one.

The coordinators, like the legislators, did not compete with the other players for points, but served as distributors. They distributed points to the players, kept track of the time, and passed out chance cards and other items needed by the players. The coordinators also informed the players of the legislative decisions by writing them on the blackboard as they were made. A detailed explanation of the duties of each coordinator was given before the game was played.

Some Highlights of the Reconstruction Game

The legislature met and began to develop the legal outlines for the reconstruction of the South as the class began playing the game. Each legislator had developed his own particular reconstruction plan and strategies for implementing it. At the first meeting, each legislator was fully prepared to fight relentlessly for the execution of his plan. However, by forming coalitions and compromising, the legislators were able to agree on a single reconstruction plan. The imaginative and creative plan developed by the legislators called for a more equitable distribution of points in the form of jobs, education, and the political and social rights of all players.

The legislators felt that certain segments of the population were barred from increasing their points because they were unable to compete with the other players in certain spheres. For example, poor whites and freedmen were not allowed to attend public schools. Therefore, it was almost impossible for them to increase their education points. The legislators believed that if barriers such as these were removed, the players would be able to compete with each other on a more equitable basis.

Since the players' goal was to accumulate points within the framework of the legislators' reconstruction plan, they reacted strongly to those aspects of the plan which they felt conflicted with their interests. When the legislature passed a bill opening public schools to freedmen and poor whites, the aristocrats threatened to fire all of their employees who attended the schools. A number of freedmen and poor whites worked for these men as sharecroppers. However, the aristocrats soon discovered that they needed the sharecroppers to plant and harvest their crops as much as the sharecroppers needed them for employment. Therefore, the aristocrats were forced to accept the law.

The law that evoked the strongest opposition was the legislators' version of the 15th Amendment. This law gave freedmen the right to vote. The freedmen represented a small percentage of the electorate. However, because neither party had a clear majority of votes, the freedmen were in a position to swing elections either for or against the party in power. At first the other players disregarded the freedmen's new political power. They were, however, awakened to the freedmen's political importance when a Republican was elected to the state legislature. Heretofore only Democrats had served in that capacity. Outraged, the aristocrats and poor whites banded together and tried to repeal the law that allowed freedmen to vote. When this failed, they decided that at the next election they would stand at the ballot box and physically prevent the freedmen from voting. However, at the end of the round they found that they had lost a considerable number of points because standing in front of the ballot box counted for zero points. They discovered that they were hurting themselves politically by this activity.

The class discussed the game when it was over. The students were asked questions that required them to draw parallels between their Reconstruction experience and the historical plan used to reconstruct the South. They were also asked to explain why there were significant differences in the two plans. The students discussed certain legislative decisions made by the legislators in their game and suggested alternative courses of action that could have been pursued. Finally, they discussed how decisions made during Reconstruction affect us today.

After discussing the game, the students exchanged roles and replayed the game. Those who opposed the legislators' plan the most were made legislators; freedmen became aristocrats. Exchanging roles enabled the students to view Reconstruction from different perspectives.

Evaluation

During and after a game session, the teacher and pupils should evaluate the game to determine if it contributes to the unit objectives. The class should also consider ways in which the game might be improved. A number of evaluation exercises may be pursued. While the game is being played the teacher should observe to see if any aspects of it are especially problematical, and think of procedures that may help to minimize the difficulties. The teacher should also take notice of those aspects of the game that are particularly successful. The students may be asked to give their impressions of the game verbally, or the teacher may administer an opinion survey to solicit the students' opinions. An essay test may help to evaluate certain aspects of the game.

6

Since Reconstruction: Questions, Problems, and Activities

The period from the end of Reconstruction to the black revolt of the 1960's can be divided into several major subperiods. The earliest is sometimes called the Nadir, or the Period of Disillusionment, which followed the Reconstruction era in the South. It was during the Nadir that the black man's hopes born during the Civil War were almost completely shattered by the reestablishment of white supremacy in the South. When Northern troops pulled out of the South in 1877, Southern whites regained control of the states. They were determined to eradicate all of the gains the black man had made during Reconstruction, and to put the black man "back in his place." In 1896, the United States Supreme Court handed down its decision in *Plessy vs. Ferguson*, in which it ruled that requiring Negroes to ride in segregated railroad cars did not constitute racial discrimination as long as the facilities were substantially equal to those provided for white passengers. This decision established a legal basis for racial segregation in the United States.

When the twentieth century began, most black people were living in the states that had made up the Confederacy. In addition to suffering from grinding poverty, Negroes were frequent victims of lynchings and other acts of violence. Because of this violence and poverty, black people began an exodus to Northern cities.

During World War I, rural Southern Negroes were lured to the industrial cities of the North by the jobs that became available. Many blacks were encouraged to leave the South by recruiters sent from labor-starved factories of the North. Southern blacks settled by the thousands in New York, Chicago, Philadelphia, Detroit, and other cities.

Nearly 100,000 Negro men served in the army in France during World War I. They served in racially segregated units. Less than half the black soldiers actually did any fighting. Most of them served in supporting forces doing such work as loading and unloading ships and building roads and bridges.

Racial tension ran high in many of the nation's big cities during World War I. A large-scale race riot took place in East St. Louis, Illinois, in 1917. In 1919 major race riots occurred in Chicago and Washington, D.C., as well as eighteen other American cities. James Weldon Johnson, who was Executive Secretary of the NAACP at that time, called it "The Red Summer," in reference to the blood that flowed in the streets.

In the early part of the twentieth century several important Negro organizations were formed, among them the National Association for the Advancement of Colored People and the National Urban League. The most highly regarded black leader of this period was Booker T. Washington. Until his death in 1915, he was the recognized spokesman for the American Negro. W. E. B. DuBois, one of the founders of the NAACP and the editor of its official magazine, *The Crisis*, was another important figure of the time. There were also lesser figures, such as Marcus Garvey who urged Negroes to take pride in being black and who favored a mass migration to Africa. The efforts of these organizations and individuals provided direction to the Negro's struggle to achieve equal rights in the United States.

It was also at this time that a Negro literary movement began to emerge. It became known as the Harlem Renaissance, or the Black Renaissance. Important American writers, such as Claude McKay, James Weldon Johnson, and Langston Hughes became prominent during this period.

In the years before the Great Depression of the 1930's, the Negro was leaving the South at the rate of nearly 50,000 a year. His destination was the cities of the North where he hoped to be able to lead a better life.

Although the black man faced many problems in the city, he found many opportunities in the urban community that he had not enjoyed in the South. In Northern cities, he was able to vote, to send his children to better schools, and get better paying jobs. The black American attained a new sense of dignity and self-respect in the black civil rights organizations that emerged during the first part of the twentieth century.

When the worldwide depression began in 1929, millions of people lost their jobs. Everyone was affected by this economic catastrophe, but black people suffered most of all. It was during this period that black people began to desert the Republicans—"Lincoln's party." In the presidential election of 1932 many black people supported Franklin D. Roosevelt, the Democratic candidate. Like most other Americans, black people had grown more politically sophisticated and had begun to vote for their best self-interests rather than for reasons of historical loyalty. Roosevelt won the 1932 election by a landslide, and promised to provide the nation a legislative program that would offer "relief, recovery and reform." Because they were a part of the poorest segment of the population, black people benefited greatly from Roosevelt's efforts. Black people gave their full support to World War II, although they faced discrimination in it as they had in previous wars. However, Negroes experienced many gains during the Roosevelt years, and the forces that led to the black revolt in the 1950's and 1960's emerged during these critical years.

THE BLACK REVOLT

Among the factors that gave rise to the black revolt in the 1950's and 1960's was the increasingly strong stand that the Supreme Court began to take against racial injustice during the Roosevelt years. Some of the most significant decisions made by the court during this period concerned higher education. Blacks who attempted to enroll in Southern and border state universities were traditionally denied admission. In a number of cases, the Supreme Court ruled that states were responsible for providing higher education to all of its citizens who desired it and who qualified for it regardless of race, creed, or color. The National Association for the Advancement of Colored People took the lead in getting these cases before the Supreme Court.

Another historical development that paved the way to the black revolt was the epoch-making Supreme Court decision in *Brown* vs. *Board of Education of Topeka*, which the Court announced on May 17, 1954. This landmark decision declared that segregation in public schools based solely on race was a violation of the Constitution. In this case the Court struck down the *Plessy* vs. *Ferguson* decision of 1896 which had established the "separate but equal" doctrine. In 1954 the Court declared, " . . . in the field of public education the doctrine of 'separate but equal' rights has no place." Although the states in the Deep South found many extralegal ways to defy the law, the ruling gave rise to forces that culminated in the black revolt of the 1960's.

The first major event of the black revolt in the South was the Montgomery bus boycott in 1956. From this boycott, Martin Luther King, Jr., emerged as the most important black leader in the nation. Other nonviolent demonstrations, marches, and sit-ins spread throughout the South. The best-known demonstrations took place in Birmingham, Alabama, in 1963, and in Selma, Alabama, in 1965. The brutal violence inflicted upon the demonstrators by state and local police during these demonstrations made a profound effect upon most Americans.

The black revolt quickly spread to Northern and Western cities. In the city, the black man could vote, but he most frequently lived in dilapidated housing, was the "last hired and first fired," and his children attended *de facto* segregated and inferior schools. Martin Luther King's civil disobedience tactics were used in the cities, but urban ghetto residents quickly grew tired of nonviolent demonstra-tion. Their hostility and tension gave rise to the most violent racial outbreaks that this country had ever witnessed. Outbreaks occurred in cities from New York to Los Angeles. The worst one of all took place in Detroit in July, 1969. This outbreak raged for five days. During that time 44 persons lost their lives and nearly 2,000 were injured. Like the civil disobedience tactics employed in the South to fight discrimination, the violent racial outbreaks kicked off strong and intense reactions within the white community, and a "law and order" attitude evolved.

During the presidential election campaign of 1968, "law and order" was a major issue. Mayors of several large Northern and Western cities were elected because of their strong stands against "crime in the streets." While these leaders were preaching "law and order," little was being done to remove the *basic* causes of violent racial outbreaks and street crimes.

The black revolt of the 1960's is probably the most critical phase of the black experience in America. It should therefore occupy a large segment of any unit or study of the black American at any grade level. Because of its immense importance and because both the teacher and the pupils are likely to have strong feelings and many misconceptions about it, some special comments about teach-ing it are in order.

Students should understand that the black revolt of the 1950's and

1960's did not spring full blown from nowhere, but was preceded by a number of significant historical events. As we have previously noted, the liberal attitude of the Supreme Court during the Roosevelt and Truman years was an important influence. However, the black revolt has deeper historical roots. From the time the black man was first enslaved on the western coast of Africa, he has been resisting oppression. He had to be forced onto the slave ships; he started revolts while crossing the Atlantic; and many slaves committed suicide by either refusing to eat or by jumping overboard. Once in the New World, slaves often feigned illness in order to avoid work. House slaves sometimes put poison in their master's food, and blacks, such as Vesey, Prosser, and Turner, organized slave rebellions. During the nineteenth century, many blacks escaped from the South by way of the Underground Railroad. In other words, the black man, in both subtle and obvious ways, has been rebelling against oppression ever since he was taken from his aboriginal land. Thus, the black revolt of the 1960's may be viewed as a culmination of this historical resistance. *It is extremely important for children to become acquainted with the historical precedents of the black revolt.*

Teachers should be careful not to overestimate the gains that have resulted from the black revolt. Students should be led to discover that even though the black American has made some progress in recent years, he is far from enjoying all the rights that most Americans inherit at birth. Black Americans can now eat in most restaurants in the South, a few attend Southern state universities, and a small number have prestigious jobs. However, the *majority* of black Americans still have the lowest paying jobs in industry, are the "last hired and first fired," and live in run-down ghetto housing.

Students should also examine employment and educational statistics in order to discover that the black man's condition in relation to white people has actually worsened in recent years, despite the progress he has made in many areas. Most of the gains from the black revolt have benefited the small Negro middle class. Students should be led to understand that the final outcome of the black revolt is uncertain. They should become acquainted with the problems that the black man still faces in American society, and they should be encouraged to think of ways in which his situation may be improved. They should be asked to devise alternative strategies that may solve his political and social problems, and to predict the possible consequences of the strategies they formulate. Students could be given specific *cases* and asked to identify the problems in the case, formulate possible solutions to them, and predict their probable outcomes. For example, pupils could be given a case like this one and then be asked to answer the questions that follow.

> Eggs cost $1.00 a dozen at the local grocery store of a black district in a large Northern city. In the next nearest grocery store, which takes one hour to get to by bus or twenty minutes by car, eggs cost 60 cents a dozen. However, most residents of the district do not own cars. The bus fare to and from the next nearest store is 60¢.
>
> 1. How might the residents of this area solve their egg problem?
> 2. What are the possible consequences of your solutions?

The students might suggest that the residents should stop buying eggs, boycott the store, set fire to the store, or open a cooperative store of their own. Although this is a hypothetical case, the author recently visited a Northern city in which most of the local stores in the black district had been burned during a violent racial outbreak. Most of the residents had to pay high taxi fares or bus fares in order to get to grocery stores to purchase basic food items. Thus, the case is not at all unrealistic. Many of the residents of this district told the author that they preferred the local stores with their high prices to no local stores at all. Although the residents of this community were justly resentful about unreasonable prices and financial exploitation, they might have worked out an effective solution to their problem if they had been equipped with more effective problem-solving skills, resources, and strategies. Sound problem-solving skills should be major outcomes of effective social studies lessons and units.

In studying the black revolt, questions involving values and valuing should and will arise. Students should be encouraged to examine their personal values and their sources. They should be led to discover that our value systems are largely composed of unexamined attitudes and predispositions that we acquire from the significant individuals in our environment. While we as teachers naturally want children to develop values that are consistent with those of our democratic society, we cannot *give* them democratic values or force values upon them. We *can* help them to rationally examine their values and their sources, and to see ways in which their values may conflict with the basic tenets of our democratic ideology. The student must decide for himself whether he wants to make his values more consistent with those generally approved in our society. However, he must become aware of the consequences of varying value systems.

One of the basic assumptions of this book is that factual knowledge will help students to see how and why they possess conflicting values and attitudes. For instance, students may say that they believe that every human being should have certain basic rights, but at the same time they may be violently opposed to having a black family move into their neighborhood. Teachers should help pupils see such value inconsistencies and help students to resolve them. However, before the teacher can help pupils to examine and clarify their values and attitudes, he must clarify his own value systems and exemplify classroom behavior consistent with the values he verbally endorses. The teacher who preaches democratic 'values, but who condemns attempts by blacks to force this nation to live up to its democratic ideals, will not contribute to the development of democratic values in students.

One way that a teacher can help students become more aware of their values and racial attitudes is to expose them to case studies and ask them leading questions about the case. Another way is to have them participate in role-playing and sociodramas where they are required to act out their beliefs and values.[1] Case studies and sociodramas involving such things as interracial marriage, discrimination in public facilities, and the problems of ghetto residents which arise from the white community will force students to express their values and beliefs. By asking students to role-play a Southern white restaurant owner who is faced with the decision of either integrating his business or losing his license, or to role-play a white couple whose daughter announces her engagement to a black man, the teacher will be able to get the students to express many of their values and beliefs.

Opened-ended and problem stories will also encourage pupils to express and examine their beliefs. The teacher can read parts of stories that present a problem and ask the students to act out solutions. The teacher can also write his own open-ended stories dealing with racial problems and conflicts or he may use stories from several available sources.[2]

The remainder of this chapter is devoted to questions, problems, and activities appropriate to this period in the history of the black

[1]See Mark Chesler and Robert Fox, *Role-Playing Methods in the Classroom* (Chicago: Science Research Associates, 1966); and James A. Banks and William W. Joyce (eds.), *Social Studies for Culturally Different Children* (Reading, Mass.: Addison-Wesley, 1970).

[2]The following two sources contain excellent open-ended stories, some of which deal with race relations: Jean D. Grambs, *Intergroup Education: Methods and Materials* (Englewood Cliffs, N.J.: Prentice-Hall, 1968); Fannie R. Shaftel and George Shaftel, *Role-Playing for Social Values: Decision-Making in the Social Studies* (Englewood Cliffs, N.J.: Prentice-Hall, 1967).

American. The first section deals with the period to the end of World War II. The second section deals with the black revolt.

PROBLEMS AND QUESTIONS

1. What was the effect of the Reconstruction Era on the people of the South?

2. Why did liberal Northerners lose interest in the Southern black man after the Reconstruction Era?

3. Why did black people begin to move to the North in the early part of the twentieth century?

4. What benefits and problems did black people experience in Northern cities?

5. What steps did Southern whites take to stop blacks from migrating to the North? Were there efforts successful?

6. What effects did World War I have on black migration to Northern cities?

7. Discuss the treatment of the black soldier in World War I. How was his treatment in this war similar to and different from his treatment in previous wars?

8. What role did the Ku Klux Klan play in the reestablishment of white supremacy in the South?

9. What is meant by "The Red Summer" of 1919? What were the causes of "The Red Summer"?

10. What were the effects of the race riots in the early part of the twentieth century on black Americans?

11. Identify some of the black leaders and organizations that emerged in the early part of the twentieth century. What were the goals of these organizations and individuals?

12. Compare and contrast the views of Booker T. Washington and W. E. B. DuBois. Which leader would you have supported? Why?

13. Why did black leaders such as Marcus Garvey and Father Divine become popular among the black masses? Why did Garvey's movement fail?

14. What was the Black Renaissance? In what ways was it a protest movement?

15. Why did the black man lose faith in "Lincoln's party"?

16. Why did the Roosevelt administration permit discrimination in some of its emergency programs? In federal housing?

17. What was the "Black Brain Trust"? Who were some of its members?

18. Why did labor leaders resent black workers who moved into Northern cities?

19. Discuss the history of the Brotherhood of Sleeping Car Porters.

20. Why did President Roosevelt issue Executive Order 8802? What consequences would have resulted if he had not issued this order?

21. Why did blacks support the United States involvement in World War II?

22. Why did Southern blacks move to Northern and Western cities during the 1940's? What were some of the problems they faced in the cities? What advantages did they experience?

23. Why did race riots occur in the 1940's? How did these riots differ from those in the early part of the century. From those in the 1960's? How were they similar to the other racial disturbances that have taken place in this country?

24. How did President Truman's policies toward blacks differ from those of the Roosevelt administration?

25. What were the most important civil rights organizations before the end of World War II and how did they deal with the problem of racial justice?

ACTIVITIES

1. Prepare a report on lynchings in the South beginning shortly after Reconstruction. Be sure to discuss the kinds of crimes that blacks were accused of committing. Also indicate in your report the steps taken to halt lynchings.

2. Pretend that you are Robert S. Abbott, editor of the *Chicago Defender,* in the early part of the twentieth century. Write an editorial urging black people to migrate to Northern cities.

3. Imagine that you are Frederick Douglass, the great black civil rights leader. Make a speech to your class urging Southern blacks to remain in the South. In preparing your report, learn about the life of Douglass so that you will be familiar with his views concerning this problem.

4. Pretend that you have witnessed a lynching. Write a letter to your family expressing your feelings about what you have seen.

5. Imagine that you are a black soldier in World War I. Write a letter to your family about your experiences in the army.

6. In a role-playing situation, interview President Woodrow Wilson about his attitudes toward blacks.

7. Read the following historical case:

The year is 1917. The city is East Saint Louis, Illinois. Many black people have moved into the city from the Deep South. Most white workers in the city feel that black workers are going to get many of the presently available jobs. One of the major factories has already begun to hire black workers. A rumor is spreading that a group of whites fired guns into a black neighborhood. It is also believed that a crowd of angry blacks has just shot a white policeman. The white community has not yet heard about the last incident. It is believed that unless immediate steps are taken, a riot will break out.

Answer the following questions:

a. What is the main problem in this case?
b. What immediate steps would you take to prevent the riot?
c. Would the immediate steps you take to prevent the riot solve the *basic* problem? If not, what other steps would you take to prevent further riots from occurring in East Saint Louis?

8. Role-play a debate between Booker T. Washington and W. E. B. DuBois.

9. You are Marcus Garvey and the year is 1916. Give a speech to a group of Harlem residents urging them to migrate to Africa.

10. Beginning in the 1920's, black literature matured and flourished. Locate poems by such writers as Claude McKay, Langston Hughes, and Countee Cullen to read in your class. What kinds of problems did these men write about?

11. Make a report on the programs set up to relieve the poor during the depression. Indicate the ones which helped black people the most and the least. Also discuss the discrimination that blacks faced in these programs.

12. *For role playing.* President Roosevelt has called a meeting of his "Black Brain Trust." Mary McLeod Bethune, Robert C. Weaver, and William H. Hastie are among the black leaders present. President Roosevelt is asking them to advise him on the major problems concerning black Americans and wants their suggestions as to the best way to solve these problems.

13. Read the following historical case:

The year is 1941. The United States is preparing for World War II. Many factory jobs have opened up because a large amount of war material is needed. However, most factories that are manufacturing war materials for the government are only hiring white workers. Many black people have moved to Northern cities in order to get jobs in these factories. Black leaders feel that industries that have government contracts should hire workers without regard to race or color. President Roosevelt has not taken a public position on this issue.

Answer the following questions:

  a. What is the main problem in this case?
  b. How do you think that it can best be solved?
  c. What are the possible consequences of your solution?
  d. What difficulties would be encountered if your solution was carried out? How might these difficulties be overcome?

14. The year is 1942. Mr. and Mrs. Alfred B. Smith moved from Clear Water, Mississippi, to Chicago so that Mr. Smith could get a job in a factory that makes war materials. The Smiths have been in Chicago for two months but Mr. Smith has not yet found a job. They are living with relatives and have spent all their savings. What problems do the Smiths face? How might they be solved? What are the possible consequences of the solutions which you propose?

15. You are a black soldier in World War II who has come home on a two-week furlough. Tell the class about some of your experiences in Europe and answer any questions your classmates might have.

PROBLEMS AND QUESTIONS FOR THE BLACK REVOLT

1. What developments before the 1950's led to the black revolt?

2. In what ways was the black revolt the culmination of many years of black resistance to oppression? Give specific examples of events, persons, and movements.

3. What methods and strategies were used by leaders of the black revolt to attack segregation? Why were these particular tactics used? Were they successful?

4. What methods were used by whites to resist the black revolt? Why were these particular tactics used? Were they successful?

5. What tactics used by whites to resist the black revolt actually helped civil rights leaders?

6. How effective was the civil rights legislation passed during the 1950's and 1960's? What changes might have improved it?

7. How successful was President Johnson's War on Poverty? What changes in it would have made it more successful?

8. Why did black militant groups emerge during the 1960's? What effects did these groups have on the civil rights movement?

9. What is the meaning of "black power"?

10. Why did violent racial outbreaks occur in urban areas during the 1960's? Compare these outbreaks with the race riots of the early part of the twentieth century. To those of the 1940's.

11. What has resulted from the black revolt of the 1960's? What outcomes might have resulted from the use of different tactics? What course of action do you think would be best for black leaders to take now?

12. What brought about the call for "law and order" in the late 1960's? Are black Americans less concerned about law and order than whites? Explain.

ACTIVITIES FOR THE BLACK REVOLT

1. Hold an election for class president. Devise ways to prevent a segment of your class from voting.

2. Make up a literacy test that no one in your class can possibly pass. Administer it to the class and explain how such tests were used in the South to prevent blacks from voting.

3. In a class report, compare and contrast the racial problems faced by the South today to those it faced after the Reconstruction Era.

4. Make a display of Jim Crow signs used in the South to indicate which public facilities were for whites and which for blacks.

5. Pretend that you are a black civil rights leader and that your class is a group of black ghetto residents. Give a speech telling the directions and goals of your organization.

6. Imagine that you are a young black child living in the South in 1955 after the Supreme Court declared public school desegregation unconstitutional. You have been selected to enroll in an all-white school which opens in one week. Write a paper describing your hopes and fears about attending a white school.

7. Pretend that you are a Southern white reporter working for the *Montgomery Times* during the Montgomery bus boycott. Write a newspaper story on the boycott.

8. Use a bar graph to illustrate the percentage of black registered voters in the South before and after the Voting Rights Act of 1965.

9. In a class report discuss why violent racial outbreaks occur, and try to think of ways in which they may be prevented.

10. Obtain a copy of the record, "The Sit-in Story." Play it for your class. (This record includes interviews with Martin Luther King, Ralph McGill, Ralph Abernathy, and other important persons in the sit-in movement. It is distributed by Folkways/Scholastic Records, 906 Sylvan Avenue, Englewood Cliffs, New Jersey 07632.) Before playing the record, briefly describe the sit-in movement or have the students read a short selection about it. Show them pictures of sit-in

demonstrations. Ask them to listen to the record and be able to answer the following questions:

 a. What were the goals of the sit-in movement?

 b. Were they attained? Why or why not?

 c. What other methods would have been equally effective in reaching the same goals? Explain.

 d. Would civil disobedience tactics be successful today in the civil rights movement? Explain.

11. Structure a role-playing situation that involves a confrontation between black militant students and a university administration. Explain the general problem in the situation to the class. Two black militant students, representing the Black Student Union, are meeting with representatives of the university administration to present their demands. Tell the class the names and titles of the characters. Ask five children in the class to volunteer to be players. The other members of the class should be asked to listen to the role-playing and be prepared to answer the following questions (write them on the board before the exercise begins):

 a. Was the conflict resolved? If so, was the solution realistic? Effective? Why or why not? What are the possible consequences of the solution(s) derived by the players?

 b. If the conflict was not resolved, why? How might it be resolved? Formulate a solution to the problem and be prepared to act it out in this same role-playing situation.

The teacher should write each of the following five descriptions on five *different* index cards. Each player should be given the card which describes his role. The other players and class members should know only the person's name and position, and not his card role description. Make sure that each child understands his role before the role-playing begins. Give the players an opportunity to ask questions in private conference with you. The role-playing should be terminated within a reasonable time period even though the problem might not be solved by the players. Repeat the role-playing situation when desired. The descriptions that should be on each card follow:

Card 1

You are Mr. Smith, Chairman of the Board of Trustees for the university. You feel that militant black students should be expelled. You are tired of violence in the streets and violence on university campuses. You are strictly in favor of "law and order." You feel that black students should be grateful that they are allowed to attend the university, especially since many who were admitted did not meet regular university entrance requirements and a number are on scholarships paid for by the taxpayers. *Main goal:* To keep the black students "in their place."

Card 2

You are President Lee, President of the University. You have agreed to meet with representatives of the Black Student Union. You are somewhat sympathetic to the black students. You feel that they should be listened to, but should not make demands. However, you would like to retain your job and do not want to offend Mr. Smith, Chairman of the Board of Trustees. *Main goal:* To reduce the conflict without making too many concessions or promises to the students.

Card 3

You are Dr. Jones, Vice President for Student Affairs. You want to be liked by the Board of Trustees, the President, and the students. You attempt to minimize hostilities by trying to make each faction understand the other. *Main goal:* To win the admiration of the President and Mr. Smith and to convince the black students that you support their demands.

Card 4

You are Len Johnson, the most vocal black militant on campus and President of the Black Student Union. You have demanded to meet with the president of the university. You have come to present him with a list of four demands: (1) more black faculty members, (2) a black studies program, (3) separate living quarters for black students, and (4) a special grading system for black students that would make it impossible for them to get grades below a "C." You are totally unwilling to compromise *any* of your demands! *Main goal:* To get all of your demands instituted by beginning of next term.

Card 5

You are Pat Green, Secretary of the Black Student Union. You are also a militant student but less militant than Len Johnson, who is totally unwilling to compromise any of the Black Student Union's demands he brings to the President. You are particularly upset because the President promised last year to hire several black professors but to date none have been hired. *Main goal:* To get your demands instituted. However, you are somewhat willing to compromise.

Evaluation

In addition to asking the questions noted above, the teacher might ask the children to write brief descriptions for each character. The pupils could then compare their descriptions of the characters with the descriptions on the cards. This kind of information will enable the class to evaluate how well each player portrayed his role as well as how well each student observed the role-playing situation and is able to determine people's motivations.

7

Resources for Teaching the Black Experience

This chapter is divided into four sections. The first lists and annotates books and periodicals that will provide the teacher with the necessary content background for teaching the black experience. A number of documentary histories are included because of the current emphasis on teaching youngsters to use primary sources.

The second section contains annotated bibliographies and methods books. Together, these sources offer the teacher an excellent guide for selecting and purchasing books for the room or school library. Several of the volumes in this section are particularly useful because of their perceptive evaluations of books and other materials. Skill in evaluating sources on minority groups is especially critical because of the great number of books and other materials flowing off the presses to meet the market for books on the black experience.

The third section lists audio-visual aids, including pictures, murals, posters, multi-media kits, records, and filmstrips. This is by no means an exhaustive list of these sources (many of which can be found in the annotated bibliographies in section two), but a highly selected list of recent materials.

The final section includes a small, carefully selected list of curriculum materials for pupils. These materials are too unusual or too new to be included in any of the annotated bibliographies.

BOOKS FOR BACKGROUND INFORMATION

ADAMS, RUSSEL L. *Great Negroes Past and Present*, 3rd ed. (Chicago: Afro-Am Publishing Company, 1970)

This highly successful book includes drawings and biographies of black heroes and is suitable reading for both teachers and pupils. Despite its rather poor index, it is an excellent resource.

American Travelers' Guide to Negro History (American Oil Company, Room 1004, 910 South Michigan Avenue, Chicago, Ill. 60680)

This guide discusses historical sites in each state concerned with the black man's role in our history. Free upon request.

APTHEKER, HERBERT. *A Documentary History of the Negro People in the United States* (New York: The Citadel Press, 1968), 2 vols.

This documentary history of the black man in America includes a preface by W. E. B. DuBois. The first volume covers the period from colonial times through the Civil War. The second volume chronicles the black man's role in our history from the Civil War to the founding of the NAACP in 1910.

BANKS, JAMES A. *March Toward Freedom: A History of Black Americans* (Palo Alto, Calif.: Fearon Publishers, 1970)

Although this book was written for students, the teacher will find it a valuable reference. It is a complete, chronological history of the black American from his African background to the black revolt of the 1960's. Included are a number of subjects that are generally ignored in other books on this level, such as black militancy. The book contains more than a hundred carefully selected illustrations and a good index.

BENNETT, LERONE, JR. *Before the Mayflower: A History of the Negro in America, 1619–1964* (Baltimore: Penguin Books, 1967)

The material in this book was originally published as a series of articles in *Ebony* magazine. Written by a journalist, it presents a unique point of view. The author is a senior editor of *Ebony*.

BLAUSTEIN, ALBERT P. and ROBERT L. ZANGRANDO. *Civil Rights and the American Negro: A Documentary History* (New York: Washington Square Press, 1968)

Includes documents not found in other documentary histories. It has an especially strong section on constitutional and legal history. The civil rights acts and several desegregation cases are included.

BUTCHER, MARGARET JUST. *The Negro in American Culture.* (New York: Mentor Books, 1967)

Alain L. Locke collected the materials for this excellent book on the black man's contributions to American literature, music, art, dance, drama and other aspects of our culture. Upon his death, Margaret J. Butcher brilliantly completed the work.

DAVIDSON, BASIL. *A History of West Africa* (Garden City, N.Y.: Doubleday, 1966)

An expert on African history, the author chronicles the history of West Africa from early times to the nineteenth century.

DROTNING, PHILIP T. *A Guide to Negro History* (Garden City, N.Y.: Doubleday, 1968)

This book is an extension of the American Oil Company's *Travelers' Guide to Negro History*. It discusses in detail historical sites that are relevant to the Negro's role in American life and history.

FISHEL, LESLIE H., JR., and BENJAMIN QUARLES. *The Negro American: A Documentary History* (Glenview, Ill.: Scott, Foresman, 1967)

This book includes extensive overviews of each historical period written by the editors. These introductions are valuable. This book is a good one, but it is weak in its treatment of the black revolt in the 1960's. However, it does include a section on early Africa, a topic often omitted in other documentary histories on black Americans.

FRANKLIN, JOHN HOPE. *From Slavery to Freedom: A History of Negro Americans* (New York: Knopf, 1967); also available in a paperback edition (New York: Vintage Books, 1969)

The classic general history of the black American.

FRANKLIN, JOHN HOPE and ISIDORE STARR. *The Negro in Twentieth Century America: A Reader on the Struggle for Civil Rights* (New York: Vintage Books, 1967)

An interesting and highly readable collection of documents on the black man's struggle in this century.

GOLDSTON, ROBERT. *The Negro Revolution* (New York: Macmillan, 1968)

Intended for young readers, this beautifully written account of the Negro's pilgrimage in America will be enjoyable and informative reading for the teacher as well.

GRANT, JOANNE. *Black Protest: History, Documents, and Analyses* (New York: Fawcett Publications, 1968)

This book includes documents from 1619 to the present. It has an especially strong section on black power.

HUGHES, LANGSTON and MILTON MELTZER. *A Pictorial History of the Negro in America* (New York: Crown Publishers, 1968)

The history of the black man in America is beautifully told in more than 1,000 prints, engravings and photographs. As valuable for the teacher as for the pupil. This excellent book is now in its twelfth printing.

International Library of Negro Life and History (New York: Publishers Company, 1967, 1968)

A library of ten volumes produced under the auspices of the Association for the Study of Negro Life and History to treat in detail the cultural and historical background of the black American. Titles in the library are:

Anthology of the American Negro in the Theatre

Historical Negro Biographies

The History of the Negro in Medicine

I, Too, Am an American—A Documentary History

Negro Americans in the Civil War

The Negro in American Literature

The Negro in Music and Art

The Negro in Sports—The Upsurge

The Negro in the United States Prior to the Civil War—On the Road to Freedom

The Negro in the United States Since the Civil War—Freedom to the Free

The Journal of Negro History (Published quarterly by the Association for the Study of Negro Life and History, 1538 Ninth Street, N.W., Washington, D.C.)

This journal contains scholarly articles on Negro history and culture, important documents, and book reviews. The Association also publishes *The Negro History Bulletin*.

KATZ, WILLIAM LOREN (General Editor). *The American Negro: His History and Literature* (New York: Arno Press, 1968)

A collection of 45 books on black history and literature. Recommended for school and public libraries.

LINCOLN, C. ERIC. *The Negro Pilgrimage in America* (New York: Bantam Books, 1967)

The text of this book is poor, but it has many illustrations from the Schomburg Collection and other sources.

Negro Book Club Newsletter (Published monthly by the Negro History Book Club, 160 West 85th Street, New York, N.Y. 10024)

This *Newsletter* is distributed free to members of the club. It discusses the most recent books in the field of race relations. These books can be purchased by members at a reduced rate.

The Negro Heritage Library (Yonkers, N.Y.: Educational Heritage, 1966)

The titles in this series attempt to cover the entire spectrum of the life and history of the Negro American. These volumes are beautifully bound and have large print. They make suitable reading for both teacher and pupil. Titles in the series include:

The American Negro Reference Book, Volumes I and II
Emerging African Nations and Their Leaders, Volumes I and II
A Martin Luther King Treasury
Negro Heritage Reader for Young People
Negroes in Public Affairs and Government
Profiles of Negro Womanhood, Volumes I and II
The Winding Road to Freedom

OSOFSKY, GILBERT. *The Burden of Race: A Documentary History of Negro-White Relations in America* (New York: Harper & Row, 1967)

This important documentary history includes representative documents from each historical period. The documents range from a description of a slave voyage to a statement by Stokley Carmichael on black power.

PLOSKI, HARRY A. and ROSCOE C. BROWN. *The Negro Almanac: The Negro—His Part in America* (New York: Bellweather Publishing Co., 1967)

An immensely useful reference book that contains a goldmine of information on the black American. It includes an overview of Negro history, biographies of famous black Americans, and essential statistical data on the Negro. Both the teacher and the pupil will find this book an indispensable reference.

QUARLES, BENJAMIN. *The Negro in the Making of America* (New York: Collier Books, 1964)

An eminent black historian gives an interesting and highly readable account of the black man's role in our history.

Report of the National Advisory Commission on Civil Disorders (New York: Bantam Books, 1968)

This controversial report includes an excellent introduction by Tom Wicker of the *New York Times* and a great deal of black history.

SLOAN, IRVING. *The Negro in Modern American History Textbooks* (Chicago: American Federation of Teachers, 1966)

A social studies teacher analyzes the treatment of the Negro in a sample of junior and senior high school American history textbooks. This book will help the teacher evaluate the treatment of the Negro in his basal social studies text.

ANNOTATED BIBLIOGRAPHIES AND METHODS BOOKS

ARCHIBALD, HELEN A. *Negro History and Culture: Selections for Use with Children* (Community Renewal Society, 116 South Michigan, Chicago, Ill. 60603) undated
Poems, biographies, songs, and other resources for teaching the history and culture of the Negro. Designed especially for elementary school teachers.

BAKER, AUGUSTA. *Books about Negro Life for Children* (New York Public Library, 20 West 43rd Street, New York, N.Y. 10019) 1968
A distinguished librarian compiles an extensive annotated list of children's books that have black characters.

BANKS, JAMES A. and WILLIAM W. JOYCE, (eds.). *Social Studies for Culturally Different Children* (Reading, Mass.: Addison-Wesley Publishing Company, 1970)
Articles in this anthology explore effective ways to use simulation, role-playing, sociodrama, and other strategies to teach the black experience. One chapter is devoted entirely to the teaching of black history. Includes commentaries by the editors.

BANFIELD, BERYLE. *Africa in the Curriculum* (Edward W. Plyden Press, Manhattanville Station, New York, N.Y. 10027) 1968
This resource and guide was prepared to help teachers plan lessons on Africa. It includes background information as well as teaching activities. It discusses the ancient African empires, African cultural patterns, literature, and arts. A valuable resource.

GIBSON, JOHN S. *The Intergroup Relations Curriculum: A Program for Elementary School Education* (The Lincoln Filene Center for Citizenship and Public Affairs, Tufts University, Medford, Mass. 02155) 1968
A comprehensive intergroup education program designed for grades K-6.

The History of the Negro in America (Berkeley Unified School District, 1414 Walnut Street, Berkeley, California) 1967
An excellent resource unit that contains comprehensive annotated bibliographies for both the teacher and pupils. Highly recommended.

Integrated School Books (NAACP Special Contribution Fund, 1790 Broadway, New York, N.Y. 10019) 1967
A list of 399 primary and elementary school texts and story books recommended by the NAACP Education Department. Annotated.

Interracial Books for Children (Council on Interracial Books for Children, Inc., 9 East 40th Street, New York, N.Y. 10016)

An excellent quarterly that includes articles, reviews, and lists of books about black Americans for children. Many of the articles are written by authors and illustrators of children books.

JACKSON, MILES M. *A Bibliography of Negro History and Culture for Young People* (Pittsburgh: University of Pittsburgh Press, 1969)
An annotated list of references for young readers.

KATZ, WILLIAM L. *Teacher's Guide to American Negro History* (Chicago: Quadrangle Books, 1968)
This useful guide includes a brief overview of Negro history, and extensive annotated bibliographies of books and other sources.

KOBLITZ, MINNIE W. *The Negro in Schoolroom Literature: Resource Materials for the Teacher of Kindergarten Through Sixth Grade* (The Center for Urban Education, 33 West 42nd Street, New York, N.Y. 10036) 1967
An excellent list of fiction, reading series, and biography that deals with black Americans. The author's discussion of each entry is helpful.

MILLENDER, DHARATHULA H. *Real Negroes/Honest Settings: Children's and Young People's Books about Negro Life and History* (American Federation of Teachers, 716 North Rush Street, Chicago, Ill. 60611) 1967
A school librarian compiles and discusses a list of fiction, biography and factual books about Negroes. The author lists the books according to recommended grade level. Illustrated.

MILLER, ELIZABETH W. *The Negro in America: A Bibliography* (Cambridge, Mass.: Harvard University Press, 1968)
Annotated list of over 3,500 books, documents, articles, and pamphlets, most of which were published since 1954. Comprehensive and useful.

ROLLINS, CHARLEMAE. *We Build Together* (National Council of Teachers of English, 508 South 6th Street, Champaign, Ill. 61820) 1967
A highly selected list of fiction, history, biography, poetry, folklore, music, science, sports, and easy-to-read books that deal with black Americans. The introduction includes a brief history of the Negro in children's books and delineates criteria for judging books about black Americans. First published in 1941. Annotated. Highly recommended.

SALK, ERWIN A. *A Layman's Guide to Negro History* (New York: McGraw-Hill, 1967)
A comprehensive, annotated list of books and teaching aids, as

well as significant information categorized under different topics. A highly valuable resource for the classroom teacher.

WELSCH, EDWIN K. *The Negro in the United States: A Research Guide* (Bloomington: Indiana University Press, 1966)
A guide for the scholar who wants to probe deeply into Negro history. Each entry is discussed in detail.

AUDIO-VISUAL AIDS

Afro-American Audio-Visual History and Culture Series (Produced and distributed by Buckingham Enterprises Incorporated, 160-08 Jamaica Avenue, Jamaica, N.Y. 11432)
A series of kits for teaching black history. Each kit contains large drawings of outstanding black Americans, a teacher's manual, texts and workbooks for the pupils, filmstrips, and recordings. Kits now available are Afro-American Architects of Our Culture, Afro-Americans in Politics, and Afro-Americans in Our History.

Afro-American History and Culture (Produced and distributed by Folkways/Scholastic Records, 906 Sylvan Avenue, Englewood Cliffs, N.J. 07632)
A set of 27 albums in five units. The history of the Negro is told largely by those who made it. Albums include: The Glory of Negro History, written and narrated by Langston Hughes; Anthology of Negro Poets in the United States; and Folk Tales from West Africa. Accompanying booklets. These albums contain a treasure of "live" information.

Afro-American History Posters (Produced and distributed by Pittman Publishing Corporation, 20 East 46th Street, New York, N.Y.)
A set of fifteen 22" x 28" multi-picture posters that depict the black man's role in the building of America.

Afro-American History Program (Produced and distributed by Educational Division, Encyclopedia Britannica, 425 North Michigan Avenue, Chicago, Illinois)
Four sets of color filmstrips (six filmstrips in each set) covering the history of the black American from slavery through the black revolt today. Textbooks are available to accompany the filmstrips. Benjamin Quarles was collaborator of the series; Sterling Stuckey served as consultant.

Afro-American History Series (AEVAC Social Studies Transparencies, produced and distributed by AEVAC, Inc., Educational Publishers, 500 Fifth Avenue, New York, N.Y. 10036)
This set of 18 full-color transparencies with 49 overlays presents

the history of the black man in America from colonial times to the present day.

Afro-American Posters (Distributed by Afro-American Posters, 1425 Fillmore Street, San Francisco, Cal. 94115)

Beautiful wall-sized portraits (black and white drawings) of such black leaders as H. Rap Brown, W. E. B. DuBois, and Stokley Carmichael.

Aime Records (Distributed by Aime Associates, Inc., 123 Manhattan Avenue, New York, N.Y. 10025)

A collection of records on various phases of Afro-American history and culture. Free brochure upon request.

Black History. (Produced and distributed by Multi-Media Productions, 580 College Ave., Palo Alto, Cal.)

A series of 15 filmstrips in vibrant colors. Each lesson includes review exercises and answers. Although this series is expensive, it is excellently done.

Ellis Photographs and Drawings (Ellis Book Store, 6447 South Cottage Grove, Chicago, Ill. 60637)

An outstanding collection of wall-sized photographs and drawings of eminent black Americans such as W. E. B. DuBois, Martin Luther King, Malcolm X, and Stokley Carmichael. Free catalogue upon request.

JEFFERSON, LOUISE E. and JAMES H. ROBINSON. *Twentieth Century Americans of Negro Lineage* (Published and distributed by Friendship Press, 475 Riverside Drive, New York, N.Y. 10027; also by Vaughn's Book Store, 12123 Dexter, Detroit, Mich. 48206)

This set consists of a portfolio of 24 photographs (10⅜″ x 14″) and a pictomap by Louise E. Jefferson. The wall-sized pictomap tells the story of the Negro's role in our history with pictures and illustrations by the author. The pictomap is also available in desk-size for pupils. The resource pamphlet that accompanies the pictomap was written by James H. Robinson. It is excellently done. This visual kit is highly recommended.

The Negro Freedom Movement: Past and Present (Wayne County Intermediate School District Desegregation Advisory Project, 1500 Guardian Building, Detroit, Mich. 48226) 1967

An excellent, comprehensive, annotated bibliography of adult and children's books and audio-visual aids. Highly recommended.

Negro History: Multi-Media Kit (Distributed by Society for Visual Education, Inc., 1345 Diversey Parkway, Chicago, Ill. 60614)

This set includes 7 sound filmstrips, 4 records, one book (Russel

L. Adams, *Great Negroes Past and Present*), three sets of picture portfolios by Winslow, Ross, and Adams, and 6 overhead transparencies. A worthwhile collection of teaching aids, although the book and portfolios could be purchased inexpensively from their publisher without buying this rather expensive kit.

Photopak (Produced and distributed by Johnson Publishing Company, 1820 South Michigan Ave., Chicago, Ill. 60616)

A collection of black and white wall-sized photographs of famous black Americans, as well as photographs of everyday black Americans at work and play.

A Picture History of the American Negro (Distributed by Rand McNally Company, Box 7600, Chicago, Illinois; and by local Pepsi Cola Bottling Companies)

This visual kit consists of a wall-sized mural chronicling the history of the black man in America that includes the portraits of 68 famous Americans drawn by Carl Owens; a student's booklet, *The American Negro: A History in Biography and Pictures* by Norman McRae and Jerry Blocker; and a teacher's manual by Norman McRae. The mural is excellently and strikingly done. Pepsi Cola distributes it free as a part of their public relations package on black history. Also in the Pepsi Cola package on black history are two sound filmstrips, *Adventures in Negro History I and II*. Although these filmstrips present a very glossy version of black history, they can be used to show pupils how different accounts of history can be written.

Which Way to Equality: The Afro-American Experience (Produced and distributed by Scholastic Magazines, 906 Sylvan Avenue, Englewood Cliffs, N. J. 07632)

Includes a teacher's guide, 36 copies of the booklets, "The Roots of Prejudice," and "Which Way to Equality (A Brief History of the Negro"); a record, "The Glory of Negro History," narrated by Langston Hughes; a filmstrip with a guide, "The Negro in U.S. History"; and a report "Teaching about the Negro in U.S. History." Reasonably priced.

WINSLOW, EUGENE, DAVID P. ROSS, and RUSSEL L. ADAMS. *Afro-Am Portfolios 1, 2, and 3* (Produced and distributed by Afro-Am Publishing Company, Inc., 1727 South Indiana Avenue, Chicago, Ill. 60616. Also distributed by the Society for Visual Education, 1345 Diversey Parkway, Chicago, Ill. 60614, as part of their *Negro History: Multi-Media Kit*)

This set of three portfolios was designed to accompany the book by Adams, *Great Negroes Past and Present*. Each set contains 24 wall-sized laminated portraits drawn by Eugene Winslow, with a brief biography on each portrait written by Russel L. Adams. The sets are titled, "Negroes in Our History," "Modern Negro Contributors," and "Negroes of Achievement 1865–1919." Here are three sets of excellent portraits produced before black history came into vogue. They are highly recommended and can be used with or without the book by Adams.

CURRICULUM MATERIALS FOR PUPILS

Call Them Heroes (Park Ridge, Ill., Silver Burdett, 1965)
A series of paperbacks developed by the Board of Education of the City of New York dealing with black and white individuals who have achieved despite barriers. These are not famous people but everyday men and women who have overcome great odds and made substantial contributions to their communities. Youngsters will perhaps be more likely to identify with these people than with more well-known persons. Includes teacher's manuals.

Doubleday Zenith Books: A Series about Minority Groups (Garden City, N.Y.: Doubleday School and Library Division, 1965)
This is an outstanding series of books about minority groups available in paperback and hardbound editions. They are excellently written, well researched, and beautifully illustrated. Currently, nine titles deal with black Americans. Authors include Basil Davidson, Benjamin Qualres, Milton Meltzer, and August Meier. John Hope Franklin served as a consultant in developing some of the titles. Includes teacher's manuals.

GEORGIADY, NICHOLAS, LOUIS G. ROMANO, ROBERT L. GREEN, and JAMES T. TALL. *Great American Negro Series* (Milwaukee: Franklin Publishers, 1968, 1969)
Sixty individual biographies of great black Americans in paperback. The creative teacher will find an infinite number of ways to use this highly flexible set of biographies, which are scrupulously researched and well written. Reasonably priced.

GILES, LUCILLE H. and LOUIS P. HOLMES. *Color Me Brown: Story-Coloring Book* (Chicago: Johnson Publishing Company, 1965)
Youngsters will surely enjoy coloring these famous black heroes and reading the brief biographies written in verse. A delightful book.

Golden Legacy: Illustrated History Magazine (Distributed free by Market Development, The Coca-Cola Company, Box 1734, Atlanta, Georgia), 1968

Each of these magazines presents, in comic-book style and format, incidents from the lives of famous black Americans, such as Harriet Tubman, Cripus Attucks, and Marcus Garvey. Youngsters will find these stories exciting, especially the reluctant readers.

HINES, JOHN. *Boyhood Adventures of Famous Black Americans Series* (New York: New Dimensions Publishing Company, 1968)

A series of creative plays that deal with the childhood of famous black Americans. Beautifully bound, pocket-sized paperbacks. Sample title: "The Boyhood Adventures of Frederick Douglass." Includes teacher's guides.

Springboards Program: The Negro in American History I (Produced and distributed by Portal Press, Inc., a subsidiary of John Wiley & Sons, One Wiley Drive, Somerset, N.J. 08873)

A reading program of high-interest materials on various subjects designed to motivate the slow reader. The set on black history includes 20 copies each of 20 titles, boxed, with a teacher's manual, concept chart, and a textbook reference chart.